CAKE DAYS

the hummingbird bakery

the hummingbird bakery

CAKE DAYS

Recipes to Make Every Day Special

Tarek Malouf
and The Hummingbird Bakers

Collins

Contents

INTRODUCTION

At The Hummingbird Bakery we love to celebrate throughout the year. Whether our customers are looking for an impressive cake for a special occasion, cupcakes for a children's birthday party or a treat for themselves or a friend, we hope our cakes help make their day a little bit special.

Although many of our customers don't wait for a reason to come in and buy some cupcakes, more often than not people visit us to buy cakes for a friend or family member's birthday, or to mark an event. After starting our Facebook page, we soon noticed that thousands of people were making our recipes at home and posting pictures of their results! We realised that home baking has become popular once again, bringing people together to celebrate. A cake is a wonderful, affordable way to toast good news or to cheer someone up, and *Cake Days* is about celebrating throughout the year, no matter how small the occasion.

At The Hummingbird Bakery we develop recipes that reflect how we feel as the year progresses and we always use seasonal ingredients. For us, the beginning of the year means preparing for Valentine's Day, with lots of colourful cupcakes to chase away the cold and treats for couples to share. We sell rich, indulgent, chocolaty Daily Specials during these chilly days – little luxuries to keep people happy until spring arrives.

As the days get longer, our Daily Specials and creations become more floral and fruity, taking advantage of the seasonal goodies that are readily available at this time. Last spring we launched our flower blossom and floral cupcakes range (see pages 38–41 and pages 68–71), which our customers loved and are perfect as Mother's Day presents. Our late-summer Specials let us be a little wilder with our imagination, using sweets, candies, sodas and other childhood favourites as our inspiration (see pages 112 and 139).

Birthdays and anniversaries often bring people into the bakeries and in this book you will find some easy cakes, cookies and whoopie pies that always create excitement at parties, plus some amazing layer cakes that many of our fans love to bake. Our three- or four-layer cakes take a little longer but are well worth the extra effort. But birthdays aren't just about children and our cocktail cupcakes are delicious alcoholic indulgences for grown-ups.

When autumn arrives, we turn our attention to Halloween and Bonfire night. Since we first opened in 2002, Halloween has become a much-loved event in Britain and our themed cupcakes, cheesecakes and pumpkin goodies fly off the shelves! As Christmas approaches our offerings become more fragrant with nutmeg, cinnamon, nuts and chocolate. We enjoy decorating our cupcakes with handmade Christmas decorations, and love watching our customers buying boxes to give as festive gifts.

I hope you'll enjoy baking from our brand new collection of Hummingbird recipes and take pleasure in sharing your delicious homemade cakes with friends and family.

Tarek Malouf

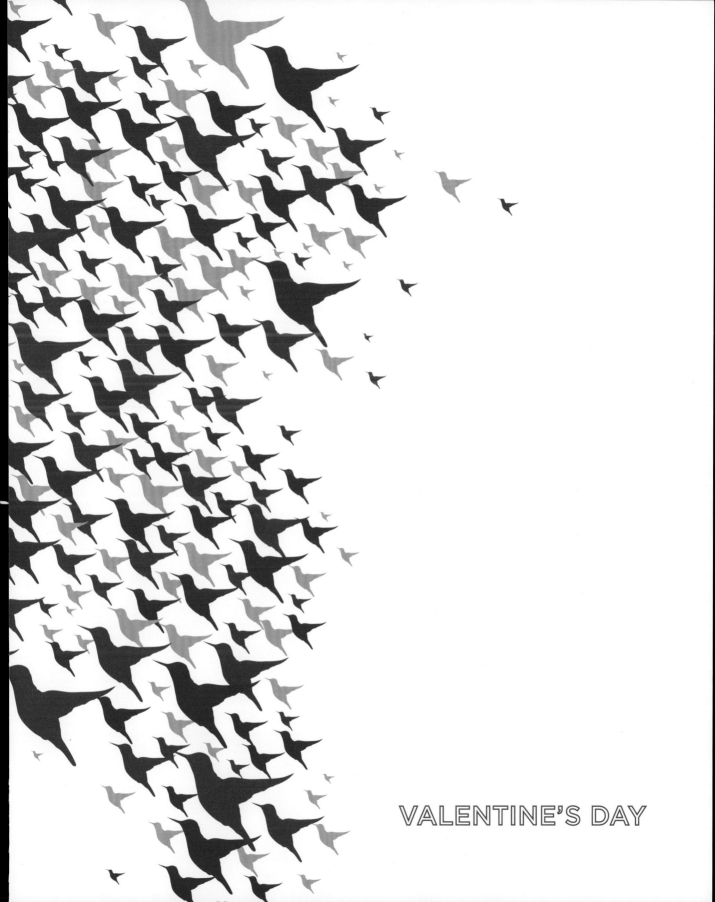

VALENTINE'S DAY

TIRAMISU CUPCAKES

The Italian-restaurant favourite recreated in cupcake form. The creamy mascarpone and strong coffee flavours come bursting through the middle of this heavenly delight.

Makes 12–16 cupcakes

FOR THE SPONGE

80g (3oz) unsalted butter, softened
280g (10oz) caster sugar
240g (8½oz) plain flour
¼ tsp salt
1 tbsp baking powder
2 large eggs
240ml (8½fl oz) whole milk
½ tsp vanilla essence

FOR THE SOAKING SYRUP

250ml (9fl oz) strong coffee
75ml (2½fl oz) Kahlúa
3 tbsp caster sugar

FOR THE FILLING AND FROSTING

400g (14oz) mascarpone cheese
50ml (1¾fl oz) Kahlúa
300ml (10½fl oz) double cream
30g (1oz) icing sugar
Cocoa powder, for dusting

One or two 12-hole deep muffin tins

1. Preheat the oven to 190°C (375°F), Gas mark 5, and line a muffin tin with muffin cases.
2. Using a hand-held electric whisk or a freestanding electric mixer with the paddle attachment, beat together the butter, sugar, flour, salt and baking powder on a low speed until the ingredients are well incorporated and have the texture of fine breadcrumbs.
3. Break the eggs into a jug, then add the milk and vanilla essence and mix together by hand. With the electric whisk or mixer running on a low speed, slowly pour three-quarters of the wet ingredients into the flour and butter mixture. Once everything has been mixed together, scrape down the sides of the bowl to pick up any ingredients that were missed, then add the rest of the milk mixture and mix the batter again, now on a medium speed, until it is smooth and even.
4. Divide the batter between the paper cases, filling them up to two-thirds. If any batter is left over, use it to fill up to four more cases in a second tin. Place in the oven and bake for 18–20 minutes or until well risen and springy to the touch. Leave to cool slightly before removing from the tin, then place on a wire rack to cool completely while you make the soaking syrup.
5. Pour the coffee and Kahlúa into a saucepan and stir in the sugar. Place the pan on the hob and bring to the boil, allowing the liquid to reduce by about half, then remove from the heat and set aside to cool.
6. Meanwhile, make the frosting. Using the electric whisk, beat the mascarpone and Kahlúa until smooth. Pour the cream into a separate bowl, add the icing sugar and whip into soft peaks. Fold the whipped cream into the mascarpone mixture, making sure it is evenly mixed in.
7. When the cupcakes have cooled, use a sharp knife to cut a piece out of each sponge – about 2cm (¾in) in diameter and 3cm (1¼in) long – and set aside. Pour approximately 1 teaspoonful of the soaking syrup over each cut-out piece of sponge and pour another teaspoonful into the hollow of each cupcake.
8. Fill each hollow to about halfway with the mascarpone cream, then place the cut-out pieces of sponge back on top of the hole, covering the filling and, if necessary, trimming the sponge pieces to fit. Lastly, frost the cupcakes with the remaining mascarpone cream and dust lightly with cocoa powder.

MOCHA CUPCAKES

On cold winter days customers queue up at our bakeries to order hot mochas from our baristas, so we decided to combine the espresso and hot chocolate flavours in a delicious cupcake.

Makes 12–16 cupcakes

FOR THE SPONGE
240ml (8½fl oz) whole milk
15g (½oz) hot-chocolate powder
5g (¼oz) instant espresso powder
80g (3oz) unsalted butter, softened
280g (10oz) caster sugar
240g (8½oz) plain flour
1 tbsp baking powder
¼ tsp salt
2 large eggs

FOR THE FROSTING
50ml (1¾fl oz) whole milk
30g (1oz) hot-chocolate powder
500g (1lb 2oz) icing sugar
160g (5½oz) unsalted butter, softened
12–16 heart-shaped chocolates, to decorate

One or two 12-hole deep muffin tins

1. Preheat the oven to 190°C (375°F), Gas mark 5, and line a muffin tin with muffin cases.
2. To make the sponge, gently warm the milk, without boiling it, then remove from the heat and add the hot-chocolate powder and coffee powder. Stir until dissolved and set aside.
3. Using a hand-held electric whisk or a freestanding electric mixer with the paddle attachment, whisk the butter, sugar, flour, baking powder and salt together on a low speed until the texture of fine breadcrumbs.
4. Break the eggs into a jug, pour in the mocha-flavoured milk and whisk together by hand. Pour three-quarters of the milk mixture into the dry ingredients and mix on a low speed to combine. Increase the speed to medium and continue mixing until you have a smooth and thick batter. Scrape down the sides of the bowl, add the remaining milk mixture and continue to mix on a medium speed until all the ingredients are incorporated and the batter is smooth once again.
5. Spoon the batter into the paper cases, up to two-thirds full. If any batter is left over, use it to fill up to four more cases in another tin. Pop in the oven and bake for 18–20 minutes or until well risen and springy to the touch. Allow to cool slightly, then remove from the tin and place on a wire rack, letting the cakes cool completely before you add the frosting.
6. To make the frosting, warm the milk gently in a saucepan, add the hot-chocolate powder and stir to dissolve. Remove from the heat and allow to cool completely.
7. Using the electric whisk or freestanding mixer with the paddle attachment, whisk the icing sugar with the butter on a low speed until the mixture is sandy-textured and no large lumps of butter are left. Gradually pour in the cooled chocolate milk, still mixing on a low speed, then increase the speed to high and whisk until light and fluffy.
8. When the cupcakes are fully cooled, divide the frosting between them, smoothing it on with a palette knife and making a swirl in the frosting. Decorate each cake with a heart-shaped chocolate to finish.

VANILLA AND CARDAMOM WHOOPIE PIES

Cardamom is an exotic eastern spice, which also works really well with creamy vanilla fillings and sponges. It certainly spices up a plain vanilla whoopie pie.

Makes 8–10 pies

FOR THE SPONGE

1 large egg
150g (5½oz) caster sugar
125g (4½oz) plain yoghurt
25ml (1fl oz) whole milk
2 tsp vanilla essence
75g (2½oz) unsalted butter, melted
¾ tsp bicarbonate of soda
275g (10oz) plain flour
¼ tsp baking powder
½ tsp ground cardamom

FOR THE FILLING

170g (6oz) unsalted butter, softened
¼ tsp ground cardamom
280g (10oz) icing sugar, plus extra for dusting
220g (8oz) vanilla Marshmallow Fluff

1. Using a hand-held electric whisk or a freestanding electric mixer with the paddle attachment, beat the egg and sugar on a low speed to bring the ingredients together, then increase the speed and whisk until light and fluffy. Stir together the yoghurt, milk and vanilla essence in a jug, then add to the egg and sugar. Pour in the melted butter and mix in thoroughly on a medium speed.
2. Sift together the remaining sponge ingredients, adding to the batter in two batches and mixing on a low speed until fully combined. Place the batter in the fridge to cool and set for 20–30 minutes.
3. Meanwhile, preheat the oven to 170°C (325°F), Gas mark 3, and line two baking trays with baking parchment.
4. Remove the batter from the fridge and spoon the mix on to the prepared trays, making 16–20 mounds (8–10 per tray), each 3–5cm (1¼–2in) in diameter and 2–3cm (¾–1¼in) apart. Place in the oven and bake for 10–13 minutes, or until lightly golden on top and springy to the touch. Remove to a wire rack and allow the sponges to cool completely before you fill them.
5. To make the filling, slowly beat together the butter, ground cardamom and icing sugar, using the electric whisk or freestanding mixer with the paddle attachment, until the butter and sugar come together. Add the marshmallow fluff and lightly mix in, then adjust the speed to high and continue mixing until light and fluffy. Place the filling in the fridge and leave to set for about 30 minutes.
6. To assemble the whoopie pies, spread about 1 tablespoon of the filling on to the flat side of one sponge, adding a little more if needed. Place another sponge (flat side down) on top to make a sandwich, then assemble all the remaining pies in the same way. Dust with icing sugar to serve.

TIP
Ready-made Marshmallow Fluff can be bought online or from larger supermarkets.

CHOCOLATE WHOOPIE PIES

This was the first type of whoopie pie that we started selling at The Hummingbird Bakery, back in 2008. Thick vanilla and marshmallow filling sandwiched between dense chocolate sponge, what could be better?

Makes 8–10 pies

FOR THE SPONGE
1 large egg
150g (5½oz) caster sugar
125g (4½oz) plain yoghurt
25ml (1fl oz) whole milk
¼ tsp vanilla essence
75g (2½oz) unsalted butter, melted
200g (7oz) plain flour
80g (3oz) cocoa powder
¾ tsp bicarbonate of soda
¼ tsp baking powder

FOR THE FILLING
170g (6oz) unsalted butter, softened
280g (10oz) icing sugar
220g (8oz) vanilla Marshmallow Fluff

1. Using a hand-held electric whisk or a freestanding electric mixer with the paddle attachment, cream the egg and the sugar until pale and fluffy. Pour the yoghurt, milk and vanilla essence into a jug and stir together, then add to the beaten egg and sugar. Add the melted butter and mix in thoroughly on a medium speed.

2. Sift the remaining sponge ingredients together, then add to the creamed mixture in two batches, mixing well on a medium speed after each addition. Place the batter in the fridge to cool and set for 20–30 minutes.

3. Meanwhile, preheat the oven to 170°C (325°F), Gas mark 3, and line two baking trays with baking parchment.

4. Once the batter has cooled down, spoon it on to the prepared trays, dividing the mixture into 16–20 mounds (8–10 per tray), each 3–5cm (1¼–2in) in diameter and spaced 2–3 cm (¾–1¼in) apart. Bake in the oven for 10–13 minutes or until springy to the touch. Remove from the trays and place on a wire rack, allowing them to cool completely before sandwiching together.

5. While the sponges are cooking, you can make the filling. Using the electric whisk or freestanding mixer with the paddle attachment, mix together the butter and the icing sugar on a low speed until well blended. Add the marshmallow fluff, and lightly mix it in, then increase the speed to high and continue mixing until light and fluffy. Place in the fridge and leave for about 30 minutes to firm up slightly.

6. To assemble the whoopie pies, take one of the sponges and spread about 1 tablespoon of the filling over the flat side, adding a little more if needed. Then stick another sponge, with the flat side facing down, on the filling to make a sandwich. Repeat with the remaining sponges and filling.

ANGEL FOOD CAKE

This is a very light, subtle cake that doesn't use butter or oil. Instead, it includes plenty of egg whites to give it volume, so make sure to whisk them enough that they form soft peaks. Serve with berries or fruit compôte.

Serves 12–16

Butter, for greasing
170g (6oz) plain flour,
    plus extra for dusting
10 egg whites
1 tsp cream of tartar
180g (6½oz) icing sugar,
    plus extra for dusting
1 tsp vanilla essence
½ tsp lemon zest
¼ tsp almond essence
450g (1lb) fresh berries
    (sliced strawberries,
    raspberries, blueberries
    or blackberries), to decorate

One 26cm (10½in) non-stick ring tin

1. Preheat the oven to 160°C (320°F), Gas mark 3, then lightly grease the tin with butter and dust with flour.
2. In a large bowl and using a hand-held electric whisk, whisk the egg whites and cream of tartar until the egg whites form soft peaks. Sift together the flour and icing sugar and carefully fold into the whisked egg whites, incorporating about 3 tablespoons at a time, then fold in the remaining ingredients, apart from the berries.
3. Pour the mixture into the prepared tin, gently smoothing the surface with the back of a spoon, then place in the oven and bake for approximately 50 minutes or until the top of the cake is golden brown and bounces back when lightly pressed.
4. Remove from the oven and allow the cake to cool slightly in the tin before turning it out on to a wire rack to cool completely. When cooled, decorate with fresh berries and dust with icing sugar.

CHERRY CUPCAKES

Sour Kirsch-soaked cherries give these cupcakes a fruit flavour that is fresh yet rich at the same time. The soaked cherries can be bought in tins or jars from large supermarkets.

Makes 12–16 cupcakes

FOR THE SPONGE
80g (3oz) unsalted butter, softened
280g (10oz) caster sugar
240g (8½oz) plain flour
1 tbsp baking powder
¼ tsp salt
2 large eggs
240ml (8½fl oz) whole milk
150g (5½oz) Kirsch-soaked cherries, drained, pitted and chopped

FOR THE FROSTING
500g (1lb 2oz) icing sugar
160g (5½oz) unsalted butter, softened
50ml (1¾fl oz) whole milk
80g (3oz) Kirsch-soaked cherries, drained, pitted and chopped, plus extra whole ones to decorate

One or two 12-hole deep muffin tins

1. Preheat the oven to 190°C (375°F), Gas mark 5, and fill a muffin tin with muffin cases.
2. Using a hand-held electric whisk or a freestanding electric mixer with the paddle attachment, beat the butter, caster sugar, flour, baking powder and salt together on a low speed until the ingredients are well incorporated and resemble fine breadcrumbs.
3. Place the eggs and milk in a jug and mix well together by hand, then add three-quarters of this mixture to the dry ingredients and mix in, still on a low speed and scraping down the sides of the bowl to make sure all the ingredients are well incorporated. Add the rest of the milk mixture and beat again on a medium speed until the batter is smooth, then stir in the chopped cherries by hand, making sure they are evenly distributed throughout the batter.
4. Divide the batter between the muffin cases, so that they are two-thirds full. Any remaining batter can be used to fill up to four more paper cases in an additional tin. Bake the cupcakes in the oven for 18–20 minutes or until the sponges bounce back when lightly pressed. Leave to cool slightly, then remove from the tin and place on a wire rack to cool completely before you add the frosting.
5. Using the electric whisk or the freestanding mixer with the paddle attachment, whisk the icing sugar with the butter on a low speed until sandy in consistency, then slowly pour in the milk. Once all the milk has been added, increase the speed to high and whisk the frosting until light and fluffy.
6. Stir in the chopped cherries by hand, then divide the frosting between the cooled cupcakes, smoothing over the surface of each cake with a palette knife and adding a decorative swirl, if you like. Finish by decorating with whole Kirsch-soaked cherries. Add them at the last minute to avoid the colour bleeding into the frosting.

CARAMELISED FRUIT
AND NUT TARTS

You can use any combination of dried fruits and nuts in this versatile recipe – just make sure the total amount of fruits and nuts corresponds to the weight given in the recipe. We love these tarts served with whipped cream or ice cream.

Makes 8 tarts

FOR THE PASTRY

110g (4oz) unsalted butter,
 softened
225g (8oz) plain flour,
 plus extra for dusting
80g (3oz) caster sugar
1 large egg

FOR THE FILLING

210g (7½oz) caster sugar
60ml (2fl oz) double cream
6 tbsp unsalted butter
550g (1lb 3oz) mixed dried
 fruit and nuts (such as apricots,
 cranberries, raisins, hazelnuts,
 flaked almonds, walnuts,
 pecans)
Whipped cream or ice cream,
 to serve

*Eight 10cm (4in) diameter
loose-bottomed tart tins*

1. Using a hand-held electric whisk or a freestanding electric mixer with the paddle attachment, mix together the butter and flour until it is crumb-like in consistency. With the machine on a low speed, add the sugar and then the egg, mixing gently just to incorporate.

2. When a dough starts to form, take it out of the bowl and knead gently on a floured work surface to bring it together. Cover the pastry in cling film and put it in the fridge to rest for 20–30 minutes.

3. Once the pastry has rested, cut it in half, then wrap one half in the cling film and pop it back in the fridge. On a lightly floured surface, roll out the other half to a thickness of about 5mm (¼in) and large enough to fill four of the tart tins.

4. Line four of the tins with the pastry, gently pressing it down into the base and sides of each tin. Using a sharp knife, cut away any excess pastry in a neat line with the edge of each tin and prick the base of the pastry a few times with the point of the knife. Use the remaining dough to line the other four tins, then place the tart cases back in the fridge to rest for another 20–30 minutes.

5. While the tart cases are resting, preheat the oven to 170°C (325°F), Gas mark 3.

6. Remove the tart cases from the fridge, line them with baking parchment and fill with baking beans, then place in the oven and bake 'blind' for 10 minutes. Take out of the oven, carefully remove the baking beans and baking parchment and bake the tart cases for another 10 minutes, or until completely cooked and a light golden-brown in colour.

7. While the tart cases are cooking, you can prepare the filling. Place the sugar in a saucepan with 4 tablespoons of water and bring to the boil, allowing the mixture to bubble away until you have a rich golden-brown caramel. Remove from the heat and carefully pour in the double cream, followed by the butter, while stirring continuously.

8. Set the caramel aside for about 10 minutes, to cool slightly, and place the mixed fruit and nuts in a bowl. Once the caramel has cooled, pour it over the fruit and nuts, stirring to ensure they are completely coated. Divide the filling between the tart cases and place in the fridge for 30–40 minutes to set. These are delicious served with whipped cream or ice cream.

COCONUT LAYER CAKE

This cake is all about the scrumptious coconut custard filling and frosting. We always use fresh coconut to decorate, making the flavour so much better and more natural. One slice will just not be enough!

Serves 10–12

FOR THE SPONGE
120g (4oz) unsalted butter, softened
400g (14oz) caster sugar
360g (12½oz) plain flour
1½ tbsp baking powder
40g (1½oz) desiccated coconut
¼ tsp salt
3 large eggs
260ml (9fl oz) coconut milk
100ml (3½fl oz) whole milk

FOR THE FILLING AND FROSTING
500ml (18fl oz) coconut milk
250ml (9fl oz) whole milk
1 tsp vanilla essence
7 egg yolks
300g (10½oz) caster sugar
40g (1½oz) plain flour
40g (1½oz) cornflour
200ml (7fl oz) double cream
50g (1¾oz) fresh coconut, shaved with a vegetable peeler and roasted if you wish (see the tip overleaf)

Three 20cm (8in) diameter loose-bottomed sandwich tins

1. Preheat the oven to 170°C (325°F), Gas mark 3, and line the tins with baking parchment.
2. Using a hand-held electric whisk or a freestanding electric mixer with the paddle attachment, mix the butter, sugar, flour, baking powder, desiccated coconut and salt together on a low speed until sandy in consistency.
3. Place the eggs in a jug with the coconut milk and whole milk, and mix together by hand. With the electric whisk or mixer running on a low speed, pour the liquid ingredients into the dry mixture and beat together until all the ingredients are combined.
4. Divide the cake batter equally between the three prepared cake tins, then place in the oven and bake for 20–25 minutes or until the sponges are golden brown and springy to the touch. Allow to cool a little in the tins before turning out on to a wire rack, then leave to cool completely before you assemble the cake.
5. While the sponges are cooking, make the custard cream for filling and frosting the cake. Pour the coconut milk, whole milk and vanilla essence into a saucepan and bring to the boil. Meanwhile, put the egg yolks in a bowl, along with the sugar, flour and cornflour, and mix together to form a thick paste. If it is too dry to come together, add 1 tablespoon of the milk mixture to loosen it up.
6. Once the milk mixture has come to the boil, add 4–5 tablespoons to the paste and stir until the paste has become a thick liquid. Pour this into the pan with the remaining milk mixture and, stirring constantly, bring the custard back to the boil and allow to thicken. It should boil for at least 1 minute to allow the flour and cornflour to cook.
7. Pour the custard on to a baking tray, then cover with cling film to stop a skin from forming, and leave to cool completely for about 30 minutes. Meanwhile, whip the cream, either by hand or using the electric whisk, until it forms soft peaks.

Continues overleaf >

8. Place the cooled custard in a separate bowl, mixing it to break it up, as it will have set while in the tray. Keep stirring until the custard is smooth, then fold the whipped cream into the custard and leave in the fridge for 20–30 minutes to chill and set slightly.

9. Once the sponges have cooled, you can assemble the cake. Place the first layer on a plate or cake card and top with 3–4 tablespoons of the coconut custard cream. Smooth it out using a palette knife, adding a little more if needed.

10. Continue this process, adding the second layer of sponge and topping it with frosting, followed by the third layer. Using the remainder of the custard cream, frost the sides and top of the cake, covering it completely so that no sponge is visible.

11. To finish, generously sprinkle the coconut shavings all over the top and sides, leaving space if you want to add further decoration to the top of the cake. To create a decoration like the one shown in the photograph, mix your desired colouring(s) with some vanilla frosting (see page 92) and pipe on to the cake in whatever shape or style you like.

TIP

If you want to roast the coconut, spread the shavings out on a baking tray and bake in the oven (preheated to 180°C/350°F/Gas mark 4) for 4–5 minutes or until toasted a light brown. Keep a close eye on the shavings while they cook and stir them about frequently as they can burn very easily.

CARAMEL CUPCAKES

When we discovered *dulce de leche* – South American tinned caramel – we got very excited. It can be found in most large supermarkets and gives these cupcakes a wonderful creamy, caramely taste.

Makes 12–16 cupcakes

FOR THE SPONGE
80g (3oz) unsalted butter, softened
280g (10oz) caster sugar
240g (8½oz) plain flour
1 tbsp baking powder
¼ tsp salt
240ml (8½fl oz) whole milk
½ tsp vanilla essence
2 large eggs
150g (5½oz) tinned caramel or *dulce de leche*

FOR THE FROSTING
500g (1lb 2oz) icing sugar
160g (5½oz) unsalted butter, softened
50ml (1¾fl oz) whole milk
100g (3½oz) tinned caramel or *dulce de leche*, plus extra to decorate (optional)

One or two 12-hole deep muffin tins

1. Preheat the oven to 190°C (375°F), Gas mark 5, and line a muffin tin with muffin cases.
2. Using a hand-held electric whisk or a freestanding electric mixer with the paddle attachment, whisk together the butter, sugar, flour, baking powder and salt on a low speed until crumb-like in consistency.
3. Place the milk and vanilla essence in a jug with the eggs and whisk by hand until combined. Pour three-quarters of this mixture into the dry ingredients and mix together on a slow speed, then increase the speed to medium and keep beating until smooth and thick. Scrape down the sides of the bowl, then add the remaining milk mixture and the tinned caramel, and continue to mix until all the ingredients are incorporated and the batter is smooth.
4. Divide the batter between the muffin cases, filling each by two-thirds. Any remaining batter can be used to fill one to four more cases in a separate tin. Place in the oven and bake for 18–20 minutes or until well risen and springy to the touch. Leave to cool for a while in the tin, then transfer to a wire rack to cool down fully while you make the frosting.
5. Using the electric whisk or freestanding mixer with the paddle attachment, beat the icing sugar with the butter on a low speed until combined and still powdery in texture. Slowly mix in the milk, and once it is incorporated, increase the speed to high and whisk until light and fluffy. Add the caramel and beat in well.
6. Spoon the frosting on to the cupcakes once they have cooled, smoothing it on with a palette knife and swirling the frosting. If you want to decorate the cakes, spoon some tinned caramel or *dulce de leche* into a piping bag with a small nozzle and pipe on to the cakes in little hearts, or whatever shape takes your fancy.

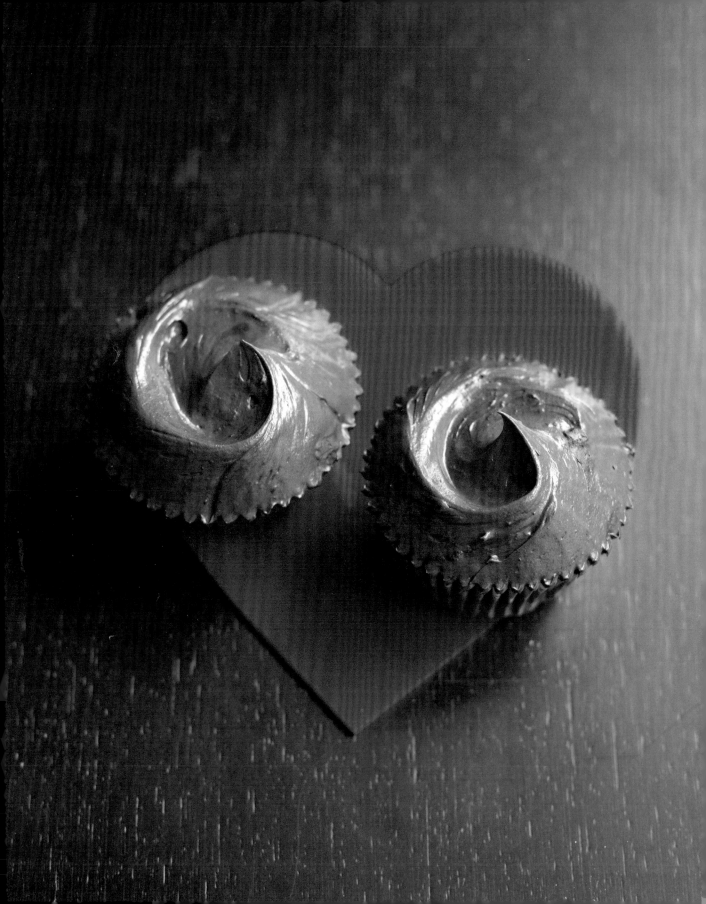

CHOCOLATE FONDANT CUPCAKES

Rich, decadent, chocolaty and creamy: has there ever been a better combination? If you want to be even more indulgent, serve with a dollop of whipped cream or custard.

Makes 12–16 cupcakes

FOR THE SPONGE
80g (3oz) unsalted butter, softened
280g (10oz) caster sugar
200g (7oz) plain flour
40g (1½oz) cocoa powder
¼ tsp salt
1 tbsp baking powder
2 large eggs
240ml (8½fl oz) whole milk

FOR THE FILLING AND FROSTING
400g (14oz) dark chocolate, finely chopped, plus 50g (1¾oz) extra to decorate (optional)
400ml (14fl oz) double cream

One or two 12-hole deep muffin tins

1. Preheat the oven to 190°C (375°F), Gas mark 5, and line a muffin tin with muffin cases.
2. Using a hand-held electric whisk or a freestanding electric mixer with the paddle attachment, set on a low speed, mix together the butter, sugar, flour, cocoa powder, salt and baking powder. Mix until the ingredients are sandy in consistency and no large lumps of butter remain.
3. Place the eggs in a jug, then pour in the milk and mix together by hand. With the whisk or mixer still on a low speed, pour three-quarters of the milk and eggs into the dry ingredients. When all the liquid has been incorporated, scrape down the sides of the bowl to pick up any ingredients that have got stuck there, then add the remaining milk mixture and mix again, now on a medium speed, until you have a smooth and even batter.
4. Spoon the batter into the paper cases, filling them two-thirds full. If any batter is left, use it to fill up to four more cases in a second muffin tin, then place in the oven and bake for 18–20 minutes or until well risen and springy to the touch. Leave to cool slightly before removing from the tin and placing on a wire rack to cool completely while you make the filling and frosting.
5. Place the finely chopped chocolate in a bowl. Pour the cream into a saucepan and heat just to boiling point. Pour the hot cream over the chocolate, give it a stir and then leave until all the chocolate has melted. Stir again until smooth, then cover with cling film and set aside to cool.
6. Place the cooled cupcakes on a board and hollow out the centre of each cake using a sharp knife, cutting out a piece about 2cm (¾in) in diameter and 3cm (1¼in) long. Set the cut-out pieces to one side, then, using a teaspoon, fill the hollow of each cake half full with the chocolate cream filling. Place the cut-out pieces of sponge on top of the filling, like a lid, trimming the pieces to fit, if you need to, and then top each cupcake with some of the chocolate cream and swirl it.
7. If you wish to decorate further, grate or chop the extra 50g (1¾oz) chocolate, and sprinkle over the cupcakes to finish.

SPRING WEEKEND BAKES

APRICOT AND ALMOND COOKIES

You might not be able to resist these cookies enough to let them cool down before devouring! For softer, chewier cookies, take them out of the oven as soon as they begin to turn golden brown.

Makes 10–12 cookies

135g (5oz) unsalted butter
80g (3oz) caster sugar
80g (3oz) soft light
   brown sugar
1 large egg
½ tsp vanilla essence
190g (7oz) plain flour
½ tsp salt
½ tsp ground cinnamon
½ tsp bicarbonate of soda
100g (3½oz) dried apricots,
   roughly chopped
60g (2oz) ground almonds
20g (¾oz) flaked almonds,
   roasted (see the tip on page 63)

1. Preheat the oven to 170°C (325°F), Gas mark 3, and line two baking sheets with baking parchment.
2. Using a hand-held electric whisk or a freestanding electric mixer with the paddle attachment, cream together the butter and both types of sugar until pale and fluffy. Add the egg and mix thoroughly on a medium-to-high speed, then add the vanilla essence and mix further.
3. Sift together the flour, salt, ground cinnamon and bicarbonate of soda. Add the dry ingredients to the creamed butter and sugar in two batches, mixing into a dough either by hand or using the freestanding mixer, then stir in the chopped apricots and ground almonds.
4. Break off pieces of the dough, about 2 tablespoons per cookie, then roll into balls and place on the prepared baking sheets. Allow five to six cookies per tray, making sure to space them evenly apart, with gaps of about 7cm (3in), as they will spread when baking.
5. Press a sprinkling of the flaked almonds on top of each cookie ball, then place in the oven and bake for 15–20 minutes or until a light golden brown in colour. Allow to cool for 10 minutes or so on the sheets before transferring to a wire rack.

LEMON AND THYME LOAF

Trust us, thyme really works in a sweet dessert. The combination of lemon and thyme is perfect – tangy and fresh.

Serves 8–10

FOR THE SPONGE

190g (7oz) unsalted butter, softened, plus extra for greasing

190g (7oz) plain flour, plus extra for dusting

Zest of 2 unwaxed lemons

3 tsp finely chopped lemon thyme leaves

190g (7oz) caster sugar

3 large eggs

1 tsp baking powder

¼ tsp salt

25ml (1fl oz) soured cream

FOR THE SOAKING SYRUP

40g (1½oz) caster sugar

Zest and juice of 1 lemon

2 tsp finely chopped lemon thyme leaves, plus extra sprigs to decorate

One 8.5 x 17.5cm (3½ x 7in) loaf tin with 7.5cm (3in) sides

1. Preheat the oven to 170°C (325°F), Gas mark 3, then grease the loaf tin with butter and dust with flour.
2. Using a hand-held electric whisk or a freestanding electric mixer with the paddle attachment, slowly beat together the butter, lemon zest, thyme leaves and sugar to bring the ingredients together, then whisk on a medium speed until light and fluffy. Break the eggs into the bowl one at a time, mixing well after each addition and scraping down the sides of the bowl to make sure all the ingredients are well combined.
3. Sift together the flour, baking powder and salt, then add to the creamed butter and egg mixture in two batches and mix together lightly. Add the soured cream and then pour the batter into the prepared loaf tin.
4. Bake in the oven for 40-50 minutes or until the sponge is firm to the touch or a skewer inserted into the middle of the loaf comes out with no cake batter sticking to it.
5. While the loaf is cooking, make the syrup. Place all the ingredients in a small saucepan, along with 40ml (1½fl oz) of water. Bring this to the boil, allowing it to reduce by about half, then pour over the cooked loaf as soon as it comes out of the oven.
6. After adding the syrup, allow the loaf to cool a little in the tin, then transfer to a wire rack to cool completely before serving. Decorate with a couple of sprigs of lemon thyme.

APPLE BLOSSOM CUPCAKES

These were sold as part of our summer floral range and proved really popular. This recipe is ideal for more experienced bakers, and variations can be made using different flower teas and essences (see overleaf).

Makes 12–16 cupcakes

FOR THE SPONGE
4 tbsp apple iced-tea powder
3 tbsp just-boiled water
80g (3oz) unsalted butter, softened
280g (10oz) caster sugar
240g (8½oz) plain flour
1 tbsp baking powder
¼ tsp salt
200ml (7fl oz) whole milk
2 large eggs

FOR THE FROSTING
4 tbsp apple iced-tea powder
50ml (1¾fl oz) whole milk
500g (1lb 2oz) icing sugar
160g (5½oz) unsalted butter, softened

One or two 12-hole deep muffin tins

1. Preheat the oven to 190°C (375°F), Gas mark 5, and line a muffin tin with muffin cases.
2. Place the apple tea powder in a bowl, add the just-boiled water and allow to dissolve completely. Using a hand-held electric whisk or a freestanding electric mixer with the paddle attachment, whisk together the butter, sugar, flour, baking powder and salt on a low speed until all the ingredients are well incorporated and resemble fine breadcrumbs.
3. Place the milk in a jug with the eggs and apple tea and whisk together by hand. Pour three-quarters of the milk mixture into the dry ingredients and mix on a low speed to combine. Increase the speed to medium and keep mixing until smooth and thick. Scrape down the sides of the bowl, add the remaining milk mixture and continue to beat on a medium speed until everything is mixed in and the batter is smooth.
4. Divide the batter between the paper cases, filling them up to two-thirds. Any remaining batter can be used to fill up to four more cases in a second muffin tin. Place in the oven and bake for 18–20 minutes or until well risen and springy to the touch. Leave to cool slightly before removing from the tin, then place on a wire rack to cool down fully before adding the frosting.
5. To make the frosting, dissolve the apple tea powder in a small bowl with the milk. Using the electric whisk or the freestanding mixer with paddle attachment, slowly whisk the icing sugar with the butter until sandy in texture and no large lumps of butter remain. Gradually pour the tea-infused milk into the icing sugar and butter mixture. Once all the milk has been added, increase the speed to high and whisk until light and fluffy.
6. Top each cake with a generous spoonful of frosting, then gently smooth over with a palette knife, adding a swirl at the top if you wish.
7. To decorate with flowers, as in the photograph, see page 246 for instructions on making shapes from sugarpaste. Alternatively, you can finish the cakes with shop-bought decorations of your choice.

Variations overleaf >

VARIATIONS

Cherry blossom cupcakes: Follow the previous recipe, replacing the apple tea powder in the sponge batter with 3 cherry blossom teabags. Put the teabags in a bowl, add 3 tablespoons of just-boiled water and leave to draw for 30 minutes. Add the brewed tea to the jug with the milk and eggs, retaining the teabags for use in the frosting. To make the frosting, first place the teabags in a small bowl with the milk, then leave to stand for 30 minutes. Remove the teabags from the milk, giving them a good squeeze to extract the maximum flavour, and mix the tea-infused milk with the butter and icing sugar, as in step 5.

Orange blossom cupcakes: Make as for apple blossom cupcakes, replacing the apple tea powder in the sponge with 1 tablespoon of orange blossom water and in the frosting with 3 teaspoons of orange blossom water. For the sponge, mix the tablespoon of orange blossom water with the milk in a jug, add the eggs and whisk together before adding to the dry ingredients as in step 3. For the frosting, first mix the orange blossom water with the milk and then mix with the butter and icing sugar.

APPLE STREUSEL CAKE

Imagine a moist apple cake ... with apple crumble on top.
Serve this with whipped cream, ice cream or custard.

Serves 8–10

FOR THE SPONGE

60g (2oz) unsalted butter,
  softened, plus extra for
  greasing
140g (5oz) plain flour,
  plus extra for dusting
100g (3½oz) caster sugar
1 large egg
½ tsp vanilla essence
1 tsp baking powder
⅛ tsp salt
80ml (3fl oz) whole milk
3 Granny Smith apples

FOR THE STREUSEL TOPPING

70g (2½oz) plain flour
½ tsp ground cinnamon
40g (1½oz) unsalted butter,
  chilled and diced
70g (2½oz) soft light brown sugar

*One 20cm (8in) diameter
spring-form cake tin*

1. Preheat the oven to 170°C (325°F), Gas mark 3, then grease the tin with butter and dust with flour.
2. First make the streusel topping. Sift the flour and ground cinnamon into a bowl. Add the butter and, using your fingertips, rub the ingredients together until they resemble breadcrumbs. Stir in the sugar and set aside while you make the sponge batter.
3. Using a hand-held electric whisk or a freestanding electric mixer with the paddle attachment, cream together the butter and sugar until pale and fluffy. Add the egg and vanilla essence, and mix thoroughly, scraping down the sides of the bowl to ensure all the ingredients are fully incorporated.
4. Sift together the flour, baking powder and salt, then add half of this mixture to the creamed butter and sugar, followed by half the milk. Mix well on a medium speed after each addition, scraping down the sides of the bowl, then repeat with the rest of the dry ingredients and the milk. Pour the batter into the prepared cake tin.
5. Peel, core and slice the apples into quarters and each quarter into three or four slices, depending on the size of the apples. Arrange the slices in concentric circles on top of the cake batter, then sprinkle with the streusel topping, making sure it forms an even layer.
6. Place in the oven and bake for 35–45 minutes or until it is golden brown on top and a skewer inserted into the middle of the cake comes out clean, with no uncooked mixture sticking to it. Set aside to cool, and then remove from the cake tin. This cake can be enjoyed warm or cold with some whipped cream, ice cream or custard.

GRASSHOPPER PIE

An old American favourite: creamy, minty and chocolaty.

Serves 10–12

FOR THE BISCUIT BASE
250g (9oz) chocolate-flavoured
  biscuits or double-chocolate
  cookies
175g (6oz) unsalted butter,
  melted

FOR THE FILLING
180g (6½oz) large white
  marshmallows
180ml (6½fl oz) whole milk
¼ tsp peppermint essence
⅛ tsp green food colouring
  (such as Dr Oetker)
700ml (1 pint 4fl oz)
  double cream
Chocolate shavings,
  to decorate (optional)

*One 23cm (9in) diameter
pie dish or loose-bottomed
tart tin*

1. In a food processor with the blade attachment, blitz the chocolate biscuits into a fine crumb. Alternatively, place in a plastic bag, seal the bag shut and crush with a rolling pin. Pour the crumbs into a bowl and add the melted butter, mixing until all the crumbs are coated and can be squeezed together.
2. Tip the crumb mixture into the pie dish or tart tin, pressing it into the base and sides, then place in the fridge and leave for 30–40 minutes to set completely.
3. Meanwhile, make the filling. In a saucepan over a low heat, melt the marshmallows in the milk. Remove from the heat, then add the peppermint essence and food colouring and stir into the marshmallow mixture until it is evenly green in colour. Set aside to cool for 10–15 minutes.
4. Pour 300ml (10½fl oz) of the cream into a bowl and whip into soft peaks either by hand or using a hand-held electric whisk, then fold into the marshmallow mixture. Pour the filling into the chilled biscuit base and leave in the fridge for 1–2 hours to set completely.
5. Once set, whip the remaining cream and spoon on to the top of the pie. You can also sprinkle with chocolate shavings if you wish.

RHUBARB AND ALMOND LOAF

Tangy rhubarb moistens the sponge in this easy-to-make loaf.
We love to eat this with a nice cup of milky tea.

Serves 8–10

FOR THE STEWED RHUBARB
4–5 stalks of rhubarb, chopped
    into 2cm (¾in) pieces
70g (2½oz) caster sugar
20g (¾oz) unsalted butter

FOR THE SPONGE
190g (7oz) unsalted butter,
    softened, plus extra for greasing
140g (5oz) plain flour,
    plus extra for dusting
190g (7oz) caster sugar
3 large eggs
1 tsp baking powder
50g (1¾oz) ground almonds
½ tsp ground cinnamon
½ tsp ground ginger
25ml (1fl oz) whole milk
100g (3½oz) stewed rhubarb
    (see above)
15g (½oz) flaked almonds

One 8.5 x 17.5cm (3½ x 7in)
loaf tin with 7.5cm (3in) sides

1. Preheat the oven to 170°C (325°F), Gas mark 3, then grease the loaf tin with butter and dust with flour.
2. Place the rhubarb in a saucepan along with the sugar, butter and 50ml (1¾fl oz) of water. Cook on a medium heat, stirring frequently, until the rhubarb softens, then remove the pan from the hob and set aside to cool completely.
3. Meanwhile, using a hand-held electric whisk or a freestanding electric mixer with the paddle attachment, cream the butter and sugar together until pale and fluffy. Add the eggs one at a time, mixing well on a medium speed after each addition and scraping down the sides of the bowl to ensure everything has been mixed in properly.
4. Sift together the flour, baking powder, ground almonds, cinnamon and ginger, then add half of this mixture to the creamed butter and eggs, followed by half the milk. Mix well after each addition, scraping down the sides of the bowl. Add the remaining dry ingredients and then the rest of the milk.
5. Stir in the stewed rhubarb, making sure it is evenly mixed into the batter, then pour into the prepared loaf tin and sprinkle the flaked almonds on the top.
6. Bake in the oven for 50–60 minutes. When cooked, the sponge should be firm to the touch or a skewer inserted into the middle of the loaf should come out clean of any uncooked batter. Allow the loaf to cool for a while in the tin before turning it out on to a wire rack to cool completely.

BREAKFAST BRAN MUFFINS

An excuse to eat cake for breakfast! You can substitute other dried fruits instead of the raisins or sultanas in these muffins, which are best eaten when fresh.

Makes 10–12 muffins

180g (6½oz) wholemeal flour
50g (1¾oz) rolled oats
50g (1¾oz) All-Bran
1 tsp finely grated orange zest
20g (¾oz) raisins or sultanas
20g (¾oz) sunflower seeds
1 tbsp baking powder
½ tsp bicarbonate of soda
⅛ tsp salt
120g (4oz) soft light
   brown sugar
250ml (9fl oz) whole milk
2 eggs
85g (3oz) unsalted butter,
   melted

One 12-hole deep muffin tin

1. Preheat the oven to 170°C (325°F), Gas mark 3, and line the tin with muffin cases.
2. In a large bowl or the bowl of a freestanding electric mixer, mix together the flour, oats, All-Bran, orange zest, raisins or sultanas, sunflower seeds, baking powder, bicarbonate of soda, salt and sugar. Pour the milk into a jug, add the eggs and mix together by hand.
3. Make a well in the centre of the dry ingredients and pour in the milk and egg mixture while mixing on a low speed using a hand-held electric whisk or the freestanding electric mixer with the paddle attachment. When all the ingredients have come together, increase the speed to medium and mix in the melted butter.
4. Divide the batter between the muffin cases, filling them two-thirds full, and bake in the oven for 18 minutes or until golden brown in colour and springy to the touch. Leave in the tin for a few minutes after removing from the oven, then transfer to a wire rack to cool down fully.

CRANBERRY MAGIC BARS

We find that cranberry works best with white chocolate; however, you may also wish to add milk or plain chocolate chips, depending on your taste.

Makes 10–12 bars

FOR THE BASE

150g (5½oz) plain flour, plus extra for dusting
40g (1½oz) icing sugar
120g (4oz) unsalted butter, softened

FOR THE TOPPING

100g (3½oz) white chocolate chips
100g (3½oz) dried cranberries
150ml (5½fl oz) unsweetened condensed milk
50g (1¾oz) desiccated coconut
50g (1¾oz) pecan halves

One 22 x 31cm (9 x 12½in) baking tray

1. Preheat the oven to 170°C (325°F), Gas mark 3, and line the baking tray with baking parchment.
2. In a freestanding electric mixer with the paddle attachment, set on a low speed, or rubbing together by hand, mix together the flour, icing sugar and butter until a dough forms.
3. Using floury fingers, press the dough into the prepared baking tray, making a slight lip around the edge to stop the filling from pouring over the edges of the base during cooking. Place in the oven and bake the base for approximately 20 minutes or until the edges are a light golden brown and the middle is pale but cooked.
4. In a large bowl, mix together all the ingredients for the topping, then spread evenly over the prepared base. Place back in the oven and bake for a further 20 minutes or until the topping is set and golden brown around the edges. Allow to cool before carefully slicing into 10–12 slices.

MIXED BERRY MUFFINS

This variation on a classic recipe uses blueberries and raspberries, but you can use other similar berries. Don't worry if most of your berries sink to the bottom of the muffins during cooking, that's perfectly normal.

Makes 10–12 muffins

300g (10½oz) plain flour
155g (5½oz) caster sugar
1 tbsp baking powder
½ tsp bicarbonate of soda
¼ tsp salt
250ml (9fl oz) whole milk
2 large eggs
1 tsp vanilla essence
85g (3oz) unsalted butter, melted
50g (1¾oz) fresh or frozen
   (and defrosted) blueberries
50g (1¾oz) fresh or frozen
   (and defrosted) raspberries

*One 12-hole or two 6-hole
deep muffin tins*

1. Preheat the oven to 190°C (375°F), Gas mark 5, and line the tin with muffin cases.
2. Sift together the flour, 115g (4oz) of the caster sugar, the baking powder, bicarbonate of soda and salt and place in a large bowl or the bowl of a freestanding electric mixer. Pour the milk into a jug, add the eggs and vanilla essence and mix together by hand.
3. Make a well in the centre of the dry ingredients and, mixing slowly in the freestanding electric mixer with the paddle attachment or using a hand-held electric whisk, pour in the milk and egg mixture. Scrape down the sides of the bowl to catch every bit of the mixture, increase the speed to medium and continue beating the batter until smooth. Then pour in the melted butter and beat again to incorporate.
4. Stir in the berries by hand, making sure they are evenly spaced throughout the mixture, then spoon the batter into the muffin cases, filling each up to two-thirds full and sprinkling the tops with the remaining sugar.
5. Bake in the oven for 25-30 minutes or until the muffins are golden brown on top and bounce back when lightly pressed. Leave in the tin for a short while, then transfer to a wire rack to cool.

MOTHER'S & FATHER'S DAY

PISTACHIO WHOOPIE PIES

The addition of pistachios makes this an oh-so-elegant whoopie pie variation. Serve them with pistachio ice cream, which can be found in Italian ice-cream shops.

Makes 8–10 pies

FOR THE SPONGE
1 large egg
150g (5½oz) caster sugar
125g (4½oz) plain yoghurt
25ml (1fl oz) whole milk
2 tsp vanilla essence
75g (2½oz) unsalted
   butter, melted
275g (10oz) plain flour
¼ tsp baking powder
¾ tsp bicarbonate of soda
60g (2oz) ground
   pistachios (see the tip below)

FOR THE FILLING
170g (6oz) unsalted butter,
   softened
280g (10oz) icing sugar
220g (8oz) vanilla
   Marshmallow Fluff

1. Using a hand-held electric whisk or a freestanding electric mixer with the paddle attachment, whisk the egg and the sugar until pale and fluffy. Pour the yoghurt and milk into a jug, add the vanilla essence and stir together, then tip this mixture into the creamed eggs and sugar and mix on a medium speed until all the ingredients are evenly incorporated. Add the melted butter and mix again.

2. Sift together the flour, baking powder and bicarbonate of soda, then add to the creamed mixture in two batches and mix in thoroughly after each addition, slowly at first and then on a medium speed. Stir in the ground pistachios by hand, making sure the nuts are evenly mixed into the batter, then place in the fridge to cool and set for 20–30 minutes.

3. Meanwhile, preheat the oven to 170°C (325°F), Gas mark 3, and line two baking trays with baking parchment.

4. Once the batter has cooled down, spoon the mix on to each tray in 8–10 mounds (16–20 in total), each 3–5cm (1¼–2in) in diameter and spaced 2–3cm (¾–1¼in) apart. Place in the oven and bake for 10–13 minutes or until the sponges are lightly golden on top and bounce back when gently pressed. Allow the cooked sponges to cool completely, on a wire rack, before assembling.

5. While they are cooking, make the filling. Using the electric whisk or freestanding mixer with the paddle attachment, slowly mix together the butter and the icing sugar until fully blended. Mix in the marshmallow fluff, then increase the speed to high and beat until light and fluffy. Place the frosting in the fridge for about 30 minutes to firm up slightly.

6. Spread the flat side of one of the sponges with about 1 tablespoon of the filling, adding a little more if needed. Sandwich another sponge on top, with the flat side facing down, then repeat with the remaining sponges and filling.

TIP
If you can't find ready-ground pistachio nuts in a shop, whole roasted (unsalted) pistachio nuts will do instead. (You will need 80–100g/3–3½oz of whole nuts for 60g of ground pistachios.) Just shell the nuts and chop them very finely with a sharp knife, or grind them in a food processor with the blade attachment or using a spice grinder, if you have one.

APRICOT CRUNCHIES

We love these fruity slices drizzled with melted white chocolate (see variation). You can substitute raisins or other small, dried fruits for the sultanas if you like.

Makes 12 slices

200g (7oz) soft dried apricots, roughly chopped
100g (3½oz) sultanas
50ml (1¾fl oz) orange juice
200g (7oz) unsalted butter, chilled and diced
150g (5½oz) wholemeal flour
150g (5½oz) rolled oats
½ tsp finely grated orange zest
75g (2½oz) soft dark brown sugar
75g (2½oz) soft light brown sugar

One 22 x 31cm (9 x 12½in) baking tray

1. Preheat the oven to 170°C (325°F), Gas mark 3, and line the baking tray with baking parchment.
2. Mix the apricots in a bowl with the sultanas and orange juice, and leave to soak for a few minutes.
3. Place the butter in a separate large bowl, along with the flour, oats and orange zest. Rub all the ingredients together by hand into a crumb-like consistency, then stir in the dark and light brown sugar.
4. Drain the orange juice from the dried fruit and stir the fruit into the oat mixture. Tip the mixture into the prepared baking tray, pressing it down into the base and corners of the tin. Bake for 25–30 minutes or until deep golden-brown in colour, then remove from the oven and allow to cool in the tray before cutting into slices.

VARIATION
To make these crunchies extra-special, try drizzling about 30g (1oz) melted white chocolate over the top of the cooked mixture and allow to set before cutting into slices.

CHOCOLATE GUINNESS CAKE

Rich, dark and chocolaty, the Guinness gives this sponge extra depth and keeps it moist. We've matched this cake with tangy cream cheese frosting, which goes just perfectly.

Serves 12–14

FOR THE SPONGE
250ml (9fl oz) Guinness
250g (9oz) unsalted butter
80g (3oz) cocoa powder
400g (14oz) caster sugar
2 eggs
1 tsp vanilla essence
140ml (5fl oz) buttermilk
280g (10oz) plain flour
2 tsp bicarbonate of soda
½ tsp baking powder

FOR THE FROSTING
50g (1¾oz) unsalted butter, softened
300g (10½oz) icing sugar
125g (4½oz) full-fat cream cheese (such as Philadelphia)
Cocoa powder, for dusting (optional)

One 23cm (9in) diameter spring-form cake tin

1. Preheat the oven to 170°C (325°F), Gas mark 3, then line the base of the tin with baking parchment.
2. Pour the Guinness into a saucepan, add the butter and gently heat until it has melted. Remove the pan from the heat and stir the cocoa powder and sugar into the warm liquid. Mix together the eggs, vanilla essence and buttermilk by hand in a jug or bowl, and then add this to the mixture in the pan.
3. Sift together the remaining sponge ingredients into a large bowl or into the bowl of a freestanding electric mixer. Using the mixer with the paddle attachment or a hand-held electric whisk, set on a low speed, pour in the contents of the pan. Scrape down the sides of the bowl and continue to mix thoroughly until all the ingredients are incorporated.
4. Pour the batter into the prepared cake tin and bake for approximately 45 minutes or until the sponge bounces back when lightly pressed and a skewer inserted into the middle of the cake comes out clean. Set aside to cool, and then remove from the tin on to a wire rack, making sure the cake is cold to the touch before you frost it.
5. Using the electric whisk or the freestanding mixer with paddle attachment, mix the butter and icing sugar together until there are no large lumps of butter and it is fully combined with the sugar in a sandy mixture. Add the cream cheese and mix in a low speed, then increase the speed to medium and beat until the frosting is light and fluffy.
6. Place the cooled cake on to a plate or cake card and top generously with the cream cheese frosting. The cake can be decorated with a light dusting of cocoa powder.

BOSTON CREAM CUPCAKES

A variation on the famous Boston cream pie, we couldn't stop eating these cupcakes during our research! Essentially a moist vanilla sponge filled with custard and topped with a rich chocolate frosting.

Makes 12–16 cupcakes

FOR THE SPONGE
80g (3oz) unsalted butter, softened
280g (10oz) caster sugar
240g (8½oz) plain flour
1 tbsp baking powder
¼ tsp salt
240ml (8½fl oz) whole milk
2 large eggs
1 tsp vanilla essence

FOR THE FILLING
250ml (9fl oz) whole milk
½ tsp vanilla essence
2 large egg yolks
50g (1¾oz) caster sugar
1 tbsp plain flour
1 tbsp cornflour

FOR THE FROSTING
400g (14oz) icing sugar
100g (3½oz) cocoa powder
160g (5½oz) unsalted butter, softened
80ml (3fl oz) whole milk
Finely grated dark chocolate, to decorate

One or two 12-hole
deep muffin tins
Piping bag (optional)

1. Preheat the oven to 190°C (375°F), Gas mark 5, and line a muffin tin with muffin cases.
2. Using a hand-held electric whisk or a freestanding electric mixer with the paddle attachment, mix the butter, sugar, flour, baking powder and salt on a low speed until the mixture resembles fine breadcrumbs.
3. Place the remaining ingredients in a jug and whisk by hand, then pour three-quarters of this mixture into the dry ingredients and mix on a low speed to combine. Increase the speed to medium and keep mixing until smooth and thick, scraping the sides of the bowl occasionally. Add the remaining milk mixture and beat until combined and smooth.
4. Spoon the batter into the paper cases, filling them by two-thirds. Any remaining batter can be spooned into more cases in another tin. Bake in the oven for 18–20 minutes or until well risen and springy to the touch, then leave to cool completely.
5. While the cupcakes are cooking, make the filling. Pour the milk and vanilla essence into a saucepan and bring to the boil. Meanwhile, whisk the remaining ingredients together by hand in a bowl until smooth and well combined.
6. Once the milk is boiling, remove from the heat and pour 4–5 tablespoons into the egg-yolk mixture to loosen, then return this mixture to the pan of hot milk, stirring to incorporate.
7. Return the pan to the heat and bring to the boil, whisking constantly to prevent lumps. Boil for at least 1 minute to ensure the flour is properly cooked. Once thickened, tip the custard into a bowl and cover with cling film to prevent a skin forming, then leave to cool completely for 30–40 minutes.
8. To make the frosting, use the electric whisk or freestanding mixer with paddle attachment to slowly beat together the icing sugar, cocoa powder and butter until sandy in texture. Gradually pour in the milk, then increase the speed to high and whisk until soft and fluffy.
9. Using a sharp knife, make a hole in the centre of each cupcake about 2cm (¾in) in diameter and 3cm (1¼in) deep, reserving the scooped-out pieces of sponge. Pipe or spoon the custard into the hole in each cake, then replace the sponge lid, trimming it if necessary to ensure the top is fairly level. Divide the chocolate frosting between the cupcakes, smooth the tops with a palette knife and add a swirl. Sprinkle with grated chocolate to decorate.

MIXED NUT SLICES

We've used a variety of nuts for these moreish slices, but you can use your own favourite selection. Just make sure that the total weight of the nuts is the same amount as we've indicated in the recipe.

Makes 12 slices

FOR THE BASE

150g (5½oz) plain flour
40g (1½oz) icing sugar
120g (4oz) unsalted butter, softened

FOR THE TOPPING

50g (1¾oz) unsalted butter
50g (1¾oz) golden syrup
110g (4oz) soft light brown sugar
2 large eggs
40g (1½oz) walnut pieces
40g (1½oz) pecan halves
40g (1½oz) shelled pistachios, roasted (see the tip below)
40g (1½oz) flaked almonds, roasted (see the tip below)
40g (1½oz) roughly chopped hazelnuts

One 22 x 31cm (9 x 12½in) baking tray

1. Preheat the oven to 170°C (325°F), Gas mark 3, and line the baking tray with baking parchment.
2. Using a freestanding electric mixer with the paddle attachment, mix the flour, icing sugar and butter into a dough. Alternatively, rub the ingredients together by hand in a bowl.
3. Press the dough into the prepared baking tray, making a slight lip around the edge to stop the filling from pouring over the sides of the tray. Place in the oven and bake the base for approximately 20 minutes or until the edges are a light golden brown and the middle is pale but cooked.
4. Meanwhile, make the topping. Place the butter in a small saucepan along with the golden syrup and brown sugar, and melt together over a low heat. Remove the pan from the hob and allow to cool slightly.
5. Break the eggs into a bowl and lightly beat with a fork. Pour the butter and syrup mixture into the eggs and stir until all the ingredients are incorporated.
6. Mix all the nuts together in a separate bowl, and scatter them over the part-cooked pastry base. Carefully pour the syrup and egg mixture over the nuts, making sure it is evenly spread over the base.
7. Bake in the oven for about 20 minutes or until the topping is set and golden brown in colour. Allow to cool before carefully cutting into 12 slices.

TIP

To roast the pistachios and flaked almonds, pop them into a non-stick saucepan and toss them over a medium-to-high heat for 2–3 minutes. Remove from the heat as soon as they turn brown as they can burn easily.

ESPRESSO CUPCAKES

A cupcake version of a perfect caffeine shot! We've decorated the cakes with chocolate coffee beans, which can be bought online or from most chocolate shops.

Makes 12–16 cupcakes

FOR THE SPONGE
240ml (8½fl oz) milk
20g (¾oz) instant espresso
    powder
80g (3oz) unsalted butter,
    softened
280g (10oz) caster sugar
240g (8½oz) plain flour
1 tbsp baking powder
¼ tsp salt
2 large eggs

FOR THE FROSTING
50ml (1¾fl oz) whole milk
16g (½oz) instant espresso
    powder
500g (1lb 2oz) icing sugar
160g (5½oz) unsalted butter,
    softened
36–48 chocolate-coated coffee
    beans, to decorate

*One or two 12-hole
deep muffin tins*

1. Preheat the oven to 190°C (375°F), Gas mark 5, and fill a muffin tin with muffin cases.
2. Lightly warm the milk, without boiling it, and dissolve the espresso powder in it. Using a hand-held electric whisk or a freestanding electric mixer with the paddle attachment, beat together the butter, sugar, flour, baking powder and salt on a low speed until they are like fine breadcrumbs in consistency.
3. Pour the coffee-flavoured milk into a jug, add the eggs and whisk by hand until combined. Pour three-quarters of this milk mixture into the dry ingredients and mix together on a low speed, then increase the speed to medium and keep beating until smooth and thick. Scrape down the sides of the bowl, then pour in the rest of the milk mixture and continue to beat on a medium speed until everything is mixed together and you have a smooth batter.
4. Divide this between the muffin cases, filling each case by two-thirds. If any batter remains, use this to fill up to four more cases in a separate tin. Bake in the oven for 18–20 minutes or until risen and springy to the touch. Leave in the tin for a few minutes, then transfer to a wire rack to cool completely before adding the frosting.
5. As before, slightly warm the milk and dissolve the espresso powder in it. Set aside to cool completely before using.
6. Using the electric whisk or freestanding mixer with the paddle attachment, set on a low speed, whisk the icing sugar with the butter until they are fully combined and the mixture is sandy in consistency. Slowly start to add the coffee-flavoured milk, then, once mixed in, increase the speed to high and whisk until light and fluffy.
7. Place spoonfuls of frosting on to the cold cupcakes, smoothing the tops with a palette knife and swirling to finish. Decorate each cake with three chocolate-coated coffee beans.

BLUEBERRY CRUMBLE LOAF

We're in love with crumble recipes at Hummingbird. Blueberries are the all-American berry, but you can use other types. As you can see from the picture, the berries will sink as the loaf cooks.

Serves 8–10

FOR THE SPONGE

190g (7oz) unsalted butter, softened, plus extra for greasing
190g (7oz) plain flour, plus extra for dusting
190g (7oz) caster sugar
3 eggs
1 tsp baking powder
¼ tsp salt
½ tsp ground cinnamon
25ml (1fl oz) whole milk
100g (3½oz) fresh or frozen (and defrosted) blueberries
50g (1¾oz) pecans, chopped

FOR THE CRUMBLE TOPPING

25g (1oz) plain flour
10g (⅓oz) unsalted butter
15g (½oz) soft light brown sugar
20g (¾oz) pecans, chopped
¼ tsp ground cinnamon

One 8.5 x 17.5cm (3½ x 7in) loaf tin with 7.5cm (3in) sides

1. Preheat the oven to 170°C (325°F), Gas mark 3, then grease the loaf tin with butter and dust with flour.
2. First make the crumble topping. In a bowl, rub the flour and butter together with your fingertips until the mixture resembles breadcrumbs. Stir in the remaining ingredients, and then set aside.
3. Next make the sponge. Using a hand-held electric whisk or a freestanding electric mixer with the paddle attachment, cream together the butter and sugar until light and fluffy. Break the eggs in one at a time, mixing well, on a medium speed, after each addition and scraping down the sides of the bowl to make sure every bit of the mixture is incorporated.
4. Sift together the flour, baking powder, salt and ground cinnamon, then add in three stages to the creamed butter and eggs, pouring in the milk after the second batch has been added. Mix well on a medium speed after each addition, scraping down the sides of the bowl once again to ensure all the ingredients are incorporated.
5. Increase the speed to medium-to-high and continue mixing until the batter is smooth and even, then add the blueberries and chopped pecans, stirring them into the batter by hand and making sure they are evenly distributed. Pour the batter into the prepared loaf tin and sprinkle the crumble mixture over the top.
6. Bake in the oven for 50–60 minutes or until the sponge feels firm and a skewer inserted into the middle comes out clean, with no cake batter sticking to it. Allow the loaf to cool a little before turning it out of the tin on to a wire rack to cool completely, then cut into slices to serve.

ROSE CUPCAKES

Another member of our popular floral range, these fragrant cupcakes (and the variations overleaf) include some slightly exotic ingredients that will delight the more experienced baker. The candied rose petals in the photograph can be bought from larger supermarkets (look in the baking aisle), specialist cook shops or online.

Makes 12–16 cupcakes

FOR THE CUPCAKES
80g (3oz) unsalted butter, softened
280g (10oz) caster sugar
240g (8½oz) plain flour
1 tbsp baking powder
¼ tsp salt
1 tbsp rosewater
240ml (8½fl oz) whole milk
2 large eggs

FOR THE FROSTING
500g (1lb 2oz) icing sugar
160g (5½oz) unsalted butter, softened
3 tsp rosewater
50ml (1¾fl oz) whole milk
Candied rose petals, to decorate

One or two 12-hole deep muffin tins

1. Preheat the oven to 190°C (375°F), Gas mark 5, and line a muffin tin with muffin cases.
2. Using a hand-held electric whisk or a freestanding electric mixer with the paddle attachment, whisk the butter, sugar, flour, baking powder and salt together on a low speed until the consistency of fine breadcrumbs.
3. Mix the rosewater with the milk in a jug, then add the eggs and whisk together by hand. Pour three-quarters of this milk mixture into the dry ingredients and mix on a low speed to combine. Increase the speed to medium and continue to mix until smooth and thick. Scrape down the sides of the bowl, add the remaining milk mixture and keep mixing on a medium speed until all the ingredients are incorporated and the batter is smooth once again.
4. Divide the batter between the muffin cases, filling each case by two-thirds. Any remaining batter can be used to fill up to four more paper cases in a second muffin tin. Pop in the oven and bake for 18–20 minutes or until well risen and springy to the touch, then allow to cool completely while you make the frosting.
5. Using the electric whisk or freestanding mixer with the paddle attachment, slowly beat together the icing sugar and the butter until the butter has been completely mixed in. (The mixture will still be powdery at this stage.) Mix the rosewater with the milk and, with the machine still running, gradually pour this into the beaten icing sugar and butter. Once added, increase the speed to high and whisk until light and fluffy.
6. Divide the frosting between the cupcakes, smoothing it over the tops with a palette knife and, if you like, making a swirl in the frosting to finish.
7. Decorate the cupcakes with candied rose petals or other floral decorations of your choice (see page 246 for instructions on how to make shapes from sugarpaste).

Variations overleaf >

Violet cupcakes: Follow the previous recipe, replacing the rosewater in the sponge batter with ¼ tsp violet essence and in the frosting with 2 drops of violet essence. Decorate with candied violet petals or other floral decorations of your choice.

Jasmine cupcakes: Make as in the rose cupcakes recipe, replacing the rosewater with jasmine tea in both the cake batter and frosting. Place 3 white jasmine teabags in 35ml (1¼fl oz) of just-boiled water and leave to draw for about 30 minutes to make a very strong brew, then add the tea to the milk and eggs in the jug, as in step 3. Retain the teabags for the frosting, steeping them in the 50ml (1¾fl oz) milk for 30 minutes before adding the tea-infused milk to the beaten icing sugar and butter. To make the flower decorations shown in the photograph, see page 246. Alternatively, you can use shop-bought decorations of your choice.

CUSTARD AND CINNAMON TART

Rich enough to be eaten on its own, we just can't get enough
of this tart. Taking the time to make the custard from scratch
is definitely worth the extra effort.

Serves 8–10

FOR THE PASTRY
110g (4oz) unsalted butter,
   softened
225g (8oz) plain flour,
   plus extra for dusting
80g (3oz) caster sugar
1 large egg

FOR THE FILLING
500ml (18fl oz) whole milk
1 tsp vanilla essence
5 large eggs, separated
100g (3½oz) plain flour
100g (3½oz) caster sugar
½ tsp salt
½ tbsp unsalted butter
1 tsp ground cinnamon,
   for dusting

*One 23cm (9in) diameter
loose-bottomed tart tin*

1. Using a freestanding electric mixer with the paddle attachment, slowly
   mix the butter and flour until they form a crumb-like consistency. Add
   the sugar, still on a low speed, then the egg, mixing gently to incorporate.
   Alternatively, rub the butter and flour together with your fingertips, then
   stir in the sugar and egg.
2. When a dough forms, take it out of the bowl and knead gently on a lightly
   floured work surface to bring it together. Wrap in cling film and put in the
   fridge to rest for 20–30 minutes.
3. Once rested, roll the pastry out on a lightly floured work surface to a
   thickness of about 5mm (¼in) and wider all round than the tart tin.
4. Carefully press the pastry into the base and sides of the tin. Using a sharp
   knife, cut away any overhanging pastry, then prick the base a few times with
   the tip of the knife. Put the lined tin in the fridge to rest for 20–30 minutes.
5. Preheat the oven to 170°C (325°F), Gas mark 3. Remove the tin from the
   fridge, then cover the pastry with baking parchment and fill with baking
   beans. Place in the oven and bake 'blind' for 12 minutes. Carefully remove
   the beans and paper and bake the case for another 15 minutes or until the
   pastry is cooked through and a light golden colour. Remove from the oven
   and set aside to cool while you make the filling.
6. Pour the milk into a saucepan, add the vanilla essence and bring to the
   boil. Meanwhile, place the egg yolks in a bowl with the flour, sugar and
   salt and mix to a thick paste. If the mixture is too dry to come together,
   add 1 tablespoon of the milk to loosen it up.
7. Once the milk has come to the boil, remove from the heat and add
   4–5 tablespoons to the egg and sugar paste. Stir until combined and the
   paste has become a thick liquid, then pour into the pan with the remaining
   milk and vanilla mixture and set over a low heat.
8. Stirring constantly, bring the custard to the boil for at least 2 minutes to
   fully cook the flour. When it has thickened, add the butter, allowing it to
   melt and stirring it in, then remove from the heat and allow to cool slightly.
9. Using a hand-held electric whisk, whip the egg whites until they form stiff
   peaks, then fold into the custard. Pour the custard into the prepared tart
   case and place in the fridge to set for a few hours, or preferably overnight.
   Leave the tart in the fridge until you are ready to eat, then dust the top
   with ground cinnamon just before serving.

CHILLI, CHEESE AND SWEETCORN MUFFINS

You can make these muffins as mild or as spicy as you like by adjusting the amount of chilli paste. Just be careful not to add too much! You can also try using other strong hard cheeses instead of the Cheddar.

Makes 10–12 muffins

5g (¼oz) unsalted butter
60g (2oz) peeled and finely
  chopped onion
½ tsp dried mixed herbs
300g (10½oz) plain flour
1 tbsp baking powder
½ tsp bicarbonate of soda
⅛ tsp salt
250ml (9fl oz) whole milk
2 large eggs
85g (3oz) unsalted butter, melted
100g (3½oz) mature Cheddar
  cheese, grated
60g (2oz) tinned sweetcorn
1 tsp red chilli paste

One 12-hole deep muffin tin

1. Preheat the oven to 170°C (325°F), Gas mark 3, and line the tin with muffin cases.
2. Melt the butter in a small frying pan over a medium heat, add the onions and the mixed herbs and fry for 3–4 minutes or until soft and glossy but not browned. Set aside to cool.
3. Sift together the flour, baking powder, bicarbonate of soda and salt, then pour the milk into a jug, break in the eggs and mix together by hand. Make a well in the centre of the dry ingredients and, using either a hand-held electric whisk or a freestanding electric mixer with the paddle attachment, start mixing on a low speed while you pour in the milk and egg mixture.
4. When all of the ingredients have come together, add the melted butter. Scrape down the sides of the bowl, increase the whisk or mixer speed to medium and keep mixing until the batter is smooth.
5. Tip in 80g (3oz) of the grated cheese, along with the sweetcorn and fried onions, and stir to combine. Lastly stir the chilli paste into the muffin batter, mixing it in well.
6. Spoon the batter into the muffin cases, filling them two-thirds full. Sprinkle the remaining cheese over the tops of the muffins and bake in the oven for about 25 minutes or until golden on top and springy to the touch. Allow to cool in the tin for a few minutes before transferring to a wire rack.

EASTER

CARROT AND GINGER CAKE

A zingy variation on our Carrot Cake, we love the four-layer presence of this scrumptious cake. It's perfect for a family gathering over Easter. We pipe on the little carrots with orange and green frosting.

Serves 14–16

FOR THE SPONGE

450g (1lb) peeled and
    finely grated carrots
2 tbsp peeled and
    grated root ginger
80ml (3fl oz) buttermilk
3 large eggs
1 tsp vanilla essence
350ml (12fl oz) vegetable oil
420g (15oz) caster sugar
500g (1lb 2oz) plain flour
2 tsp baking powder
1 tsp bicarbonate of soda
1 tsp salt
1 tsp ground cinnamon
1 tsp ground ginger
80g (3oz) pecans, roasted
    (see tip on page 63) and
    chopped

FOR THE FROSTING

100g (3½oz) unsalted butter,
    softened
600g (1lb 5oz) icing sugar
1 tbsp finely grated orange zest,
    plus extra to decorate (optional)
250g (9oz) full-fat cream cheese
Orange and green food colouring
    and pecan halves, to decorate
    (optional)

*Four 20cm (8in) diameter
loose-bottomed sandwich tins*

1. Preheat the oven to 170°C (325°F), Gas mark 3, and line the sandwich tins with baking parchment.

2. Using a hand-held electric whisk or a freestanding electric mixer with the paddle attachment, mix together the carrots, root ginger, buttermilk, eggs, vanilla essence, vegetable oil and sugar until all the ingredients are well combined.

3. Sift together the flour, baking powder, bicarbonate of soda, salt and ground spices, then slowly beat these into the egg and carrot mixture, adding the dry ingredients in three batches. Mix well after each addition, scraping down the sides of the bowl to pick up any ingredients that may have got stuck there. Stir in the chopped pecans and mix the cake batter until it is smooth and even.

4. Divide the batter between the four prepared sandwich tins and bake for approximately 30 minutes or until the top of each sponge bounces back when lightly pressed. Allow the cakes to cool completely, on a wire rack, while you make the frosting.

5. Using the electric whisk or freestanding mixer with the paddle attachment, mix together the butter and icing sugar on a low speed until combined but still powdery in consistency. Add the orange zest and cream cheese, increase the speed to medium-to-high and mix well until the frosting is smooth, light and fluffy.

6. If you want to decorate the cake like the photograph, set aside a small amount of the frosting in two separate bowls and colour with a few drops of orange and green food colouring.

7. When the sponges feel cold to the touch, spread some of the uncoloured frosting between each layer and sandwich all four together. Use the remaining plain frosting to cover the top and outside of the assembled cake, then decorate with your choice of piped coloured frosting, pecans or grated orange zest.

BLOOD ORANGE CHEESECAKE

Blood oranges are in season around Easter. Besides having a distinctive red flesh, they also have a more delicate, tangy flavour than normal oranges, which is essential for this amazing cheesecake.

Serves 8–12

FOR THE BISCUIT BASE
220g (8oz) digestive biscuits
100g (3½oz) unsalted butter,
   melted
½ tsp finely grated
   blood orange zest

FOR THE CHEESECAKE TOPPING
700g (1½lb) full-fat cream
   cheese (such as Philadelphia)
100g (3½oz) ricotta cheese
120g (4oz) caster sugar
2 tbsp finely grated
   blood orange zest
3 large eggs

FOR THE ORANGE JELLY
100ml (3½fl oz) blood orange
   juice, strained
2 leaves of gelatine

*One 20cm (8in) diameter
spring-form cake tin*

1. First line the base of the cake tin with baking parchment. In a food processor with the blade attachment, blitz the digestive biscuits into fine crumbs. Alternatively, place the biscuits in a plastic bag, seal it closed and crush with a rolling pin.
2. Pour the biscuit crumbs into a bowl, add the melted butter and orange zest and mix together with a spoon. Tip the mixture into the prepared tin, pressing it into the base with the back of the spoon, and leave in the fridge for 20–30 minutes to cool and set.
3. Meanwhile, preheat the oven to 160°C (320°F), Gas mark 3, and make the cheesecake topping.
4. Using a freestanding electric mixer with the paddle attachment, or a hand-held electric whisk, beat together the cream cheese, ricotta, sugar and orange zest until smooth. Add the eggs one at a time, mixing thoroughly after each addition and scraping down the sides of the bowl to incorporate every last bit of the mixture.
5. Pour the cheesecake on to the chilled biscuit base and place in a roasting tin. (See also the tip below.) Fill this with water so that it comes to about 5mm (¼in) from the top of the cake tin, creating a water bath (or bain marie) for the cheesecake to bake in so that it doesn't dry out.
6. Bake in the oven for approximately 40 minutes or until the cheesecake is a light golden colour, especially around the edges, and firm to the touch, with only a slight wobble in the middle. Allow the cheesecake to cool down to room temperature while still in the tin, and then place in the fridge to set for a few hours, or preferably overnight.
7. An hour or so before serving, make the orange jelly to go on top of the cheesecake. In a small saucepan, gently heat the orange juice and then remove from the hob. Soften the gelatine leaves in a bowl of cold water, then drain and dissolve the softened gelatine in the warm orange juice.
8. Allow the jelly to cool slightly before pouring over the cheesecake, then place in the fridge to set for approximately 1 hour. Carefully remove from the tin before serving.

TIP
To prevent any water leaking into the cheesecake while it is baking, place the filled cake tin on a large piece of foil and fold it up around the sides of the tin. Then place the cake tin in the roasting tin and fill with water as above.

APPLE AND WALNUT CUPCAKES

The apples in these cupcakes make the sponge really moist and flavoursome. Decorate with your preference of walnut halves or chopped walnuts.

Makes 12–16 cupcakes

FOR THE SPONGE
80g (3oz) unsalted butter, softened
280g (10oz) caster sugar
240g (8½oz) plain flour
1 tbsp baking powder
¼ tsp salt
1½ tsp ground cinnamon
240ml (8½fl oz) whole milk
2 large eggs
2 Granny Smith apples
50g (1¾oz) walnuts, chopped

FOR THE FROSTING
600g (1lb 5oz) icing sugar
100g (3½oz) unsalted butter, softened
250g (9oz) full fat cream cheese (such as Philadelphia)
Ground cinnamon, for dusting
12–16 walnut halves, to decorate

One or two 12-hole deep muffin tins

1. Preheat the oven to 190°C (375°F), Gas mark 5, and line a muffin tin with muffin cases.
2. Using a hand-held electric whisk or a freestanding electric mixer with the paddle attachment, beat together the butter, sugar, flour, baking powder, salt and cinnamon on a low speed until the consistency of fine breadcrumbs.
3. Place the milk in a jug with the eggs and whisk by hand until combined, then pour three-quarters of the milk mixture into the dry ingredients and mix on a low speed to combine. Increase the speed to medium and keep beating until smooth and thick, adding the scrapings from the sides of the bowl, then pour in the remaining milk mixture and continue to mix on a medium speed until all the ingredients are incorporated and the batter is smooth.
4. Peel, core and chop the apples into 1cm (½in) pieces (the total weight should be about 200g/7oz), then stir into the batter with the walnuts. Spoon the batter into the paper cases to fill them by about two-thirds. If any batter is left, it can be used to fill up to four more cases in a second muffin tin.
5. Bake the cupcakes for 18–20 minutes or until they bounce back when gently pressed. Allow to cool in the tin a little, then remove and leave to cool completely before adding the frosting.
6. While the cakes are cooling, make the frosting. Using the electric whisk or freestanding electric mixer with the paddle attachment, beat the icing sugar with the butter on a low speed until sandy in texture and no large lumps of butter are left. Add the cream cheese and mix on a medium-to-high speed until the frosting is smooth, light and fluffy.
7. When the cupcakes feel cold to the touch, spread the frosting on to them, smoothing and swirling the surface with a palette knife. Dust the cakes with ground cinnamon and top each with half a walnut to finish.

MALTED CHOCOLATE CUPCAKES

One of the most popular daily specials we've ever sold in our branches, we still get requests to bring this flavour back. Chocolate and malted milk just work so well together. Either use whole Maltesers for the decoration, or you can crush them and sprinkle over the top.

Makes 12–16 cupcakes

FOR THE SPONGE
150ml (5½fl oz) sunflower oil
75ml (2½fl oz) whole milk
75ml (2½fl oz) buttermilk
1 large egg
1½ tsp vanilla essence
240g (8½oz) plain flour
25g (1oz) cocoa powder
2 tsp baking powder
¼ tsp salt
330g (11½oz) caster sugar
150ml (5½fl oz) boiling water

FOR THE FROSTING
200g (7oz) dark chocolate
  chips (minimum 70%
  cocoa solids)
240ml (8½fl oz) double cream
115g (4oz) malted-milk powder
50g (1¾oz) full-fat cream cheese
  (such as Philadelphia)
35g (1¼oz) caster sugar
36–48 Maltesers, to decorate

*One or two 12-hole
deep muffin tins*

1. Preheat the oven to 190°C (375°F), Gas mark 5, and fill a muffin tin with muffin cases.
2. Using a hand-held electric whisk or a freestanding electric mixer with the paddle attachment, beat together the oil with the milk, buttermilk, egg and vanilla essence on low speed until well blended. Sift together the flour, cocoa powder, baking powder and salt, then stir in the sugar. Add a third of these dry ingredients to the oil and milk mixture and beat in slowly until evenly incorporated.
3. Beat in a third of the boiling water, followed by another third of the dry ingredients, then repeat with the remaining ingredients, mixing together until they are all combined. Remember to scrape down the sides of the bowl after each addition, to ensure a well-mixed batter.
4. Divide the mixture between the paper cases, filling each by two-thirds. Any remaining batter can be used to fill one to four more cases in a separate tin. Place in the oven and bake for 18–20 minutes or until springy to the touch. Allow to cool a little before removing from the tin, then transfer to a wire rack to cool down completely before adding the frosting.
5. To make the frosting, place the chocolate chips in a bowl set over a saucepan of simmering water and allow to melt, then remove from the heat and set aside to cool.
6. Meanwhile, using the electric whisk, whip the cream with the malted-milk powder until it forms soft peaks. In a separate bowl, beat the cream cheese with the caster sugar until combined, then add the cooled chocolate and mix again.
7. Carefully fold the whipped cream into the cream cheese mixture, adding half the whipped cream at a time. Divide the frosting between the cupcakes, smoothing and swirling with a palette knife, then decorate each cupcake with 3 Maltesers.

CARROT CAKE WHOOPIE PIES

Whoopie pies are really popular, so we've come up with lots of variations to suit every taste. The comforting, spiced flavour of carrot cake makes these whoopie pies extremely tasty.

Makes 8–10 pies

FOR THE SPONGE
1 large egg
150g (5½oz) caster sugar
125g (4½oz) plain yoghurt
25ml (1fl oz) whole milk
2 tsp vanilla essence
75g (2½oz) unsalted butter,
    melted
275g (10oz) plain flour
½ tsp ground cinnamon
½ tsp ground ginger
¼ tsp freshly grated nutmeg
¼ tsp baking powder
¾ tsp bicarbonate of soda
¼ tsp fine sea salt
100g (3½oz) peeled
    and finely grated carrots

FOR THE FILLING
170g (6oz) unsalted butter,
    softened
½ tsp ground cinnamon
280g (10oz) icing sugar
220g (8oz) vanilla
    Marshmallow Fluff

1. Using a hand-held electric whisk or a freestanding electric mixer with the paddle attachment, whisk the egg and the sugar on a medium speed until pale and fluffy. In a jug, stir together the yoghurt, milk and vanilla essence, then pour the yoghurt mixture into the whisked egg and sugar, followed by the melted butter, and mix on a low speed to combine.
2. Sift together the flour, ground spices, baking powder, bicarbonate of soda and salt, then add to the egg and yoghurt mixture in two batches, gently mixing until just incorporated.
3. Tip the grated carrots into a colander and press them to remove any excess liquid, then add these to the batter, stirring them in by hand until they are evenly mixed in. Put the batter in the fridge and allow to cool and set for 30–40 minutes.
4. Meanwhile, preheat the oven to 170°C (325°F), Gas mark 3, and line two baking trays with baking parchment.
5. Once the batter has cooled down, spoon it on to the prepared trays in a series of small mounds. Aim for 16–20 mounds of batter in total, each 3–5cm (1¼–2in) in diameter and spaced 2–3 cm (¾–1¼in) apart.
6. Bake in the oven for 10–13 minutes or until lightly golden all over and springy to the touch. Remove the sponges from the oven, place on a wire rack and allow to cool completely before adding the filling.
7. While the sponges are cooking, make the filling. Using the freestanding mixer or electric whisk, mix together the butter, cinnamon and the icing sugar on a low speed until the butter and sugar come together. Add the marshmallow fluff, mixing until just incorporated, then increase the speed to high and mix until light and fluffy. Leave this filling in the fridge for about 30 minutes to set.
8. When the sponges feel cold to the touch, spread about 1 tablespoon of the filling on to the flat side of one sponge, adding a little more if needed. Then stick another sponge on top (flat side down) to make a sandwich. Repeat with the remaining sponges and filling, to create eight to ten whoopie pies in total.

COCONUT CREAM PIE

The coconut and custard combine perfectly in this pie filling. It's well worth seeking out fresh coconut for the top. Decorate with grated chocolate if you wish.

Serves 8–10

FOR THE PASTRY
225g (8oz) plain flour,
   plus extra for dusting
110g (4oz) unsalted butter,
   softened
80g (3oz) caster sugar
1 large egg

FOR THE FILLING
4 large egg yolks
2 tsp vanilla essence
140g (5oz) caster sugar
35g (1¼oz) cornflour
¼ tsp salt
240ml (8½fl oz) coconut milk
350ml (12fl oz) whole milk

FOR THE TOPPING
350ml (12fl oz) double cream
1 tsp vanilla essence
2 tbsp icing sugar
3 tbsp coconut flakes, toasted
   (see the tip on page 27)

*One 23cm (9in) diameter
loose-bottomed tart tin*

1. To make the pastry, use a freestanding electric mixer with the paddle attachment to slowly mix the flour and butter until crumb-like in consistency. Add the sugar, then the egg, mixing gently to incorporate. You can also do this by hand, rubbing together the butter and flour with your fingertips and then stirring in the sugar and egg with a spoon. When a dough forms, remove it from the bowl and knead lightly on a floured surface to bring it together. Wrap in cling film and put in the fridge to rest for 20–30 minutes.

2. Once rested, roll the pastry out on a lightly floured worktop to a thickness of about 5mm (¼in) and large enough to line your tart tin. Carefully lay the pastry over the tin and gently press it into the base and sides.

3. Using a sharp knife, cut away any overhanging pastry, prick the base a few times, then place the lined tin in the fridge to rest for 20–30 minutes.

4. Preheat the oven to 170°C (325°F), Gas mark 3. Once the pastry has rested, cover the pastry with baking parchment and fill with baking beans, then bake 'blind' in the oven for 12 minutes. Carefully remove the beans and the paper, and bake the pastry for another 15 minutes or until cooked through and a light-golden colour. Set aside to cool.

5. While the pastry is baking, make the filling. Place the egg yolks and vanilla essence in a bowl, beating with a fork to break up the yolks. In a saucepan mix together the sugar, cornflour and salt, then add 90ml (3fl oz) of the coconut milk and whisk to a smooth paste. Pour in the remaining coconut milk and the whole milk and stir to combine.

6. Place the pan over a low heat and bring the mixture to the boil, whisking continuously. As soon as it starts to thicken, take 3 tablespoons of the hot milk mixture and stir into the egg yolks, then pour the egg yolk mixture into the pan of milk and continue to heat, stirring constantly, until the mixture is thick and looks like custard.

7. Pour the hot filling into the cooled tart base and cover straight away with cling film to prevent a skin forming. Allow the filling to cool to room temperature, then place the pie in the fridge and leave for up to 1 hour to set and cool completely before you add the topping.

8. Pour the cream into a bowl, add the vanilla essence and icing sugar and whip by hand or with an electric whisk until soft peaks form. Spoon this onto the cooled pie and sprinkle with toasted flaked coconut to finish.

LEMON AND POPPY SEED LOAF

The ricotta cheese in this recipe helps make the loaf moist and rich. We love how the little black poppy seeds stand out from the sponge when it's sliced.

Serves 8–10

FOR THE SPONGE
190g (7oz) unsalted butter, softened, plus extra for greasing
190g (7oz) plain flour, plus extra for dusting
190g (7oz) caster sugar
3 large eggs
1 tsp baking powder
¼ tsp salt
4 tbsp poppy seeds
2 tbsp lemon zest
25ml (1fl oz) whole milk
80g (3oz) ricotta cheese

FOR THE SOAKING SYRUP
Juice of 1 lemon
50g (1¾oz) caster sugar

One 8.5 x 17.5cm (3½ x 7in) loaf tin with 7.5cm (3in) sides

1. Preheat the oven to 170°C (325°F), Gas mark 3, then grease the loaf tin with butter and dust with flour.
2. Using a hand-held electric whisk or a freestanding electric mixer with the paddle attachment, cream together the butter and caster sugar. Add the eggs one at a time, mixing well after each addition and scraping down the sides of the bowl.
3. In a separate bowl, sift together the flour, baking powder and salt, then mix in the poppy seeds and lemon zest. Add these dry ingredients to the creamed butter and sugar in three stages and on a low speed, mixing well between each addition and adding the milk after the second batch of dry ingredients. Increase the speed to medium and keep mixing until the batter is smooth and even, then mix in the ricotta cheese.
4. Pour the batter into the prepared loaf tin and bake in the oven for 50–60 minutes or until the sponge bounces back when lightly pressed and a skewer inserted into the middle of the cake comes out clean, with no uncooked batter sticking to it.
5. While the cake is baking, put the lemon juice and sugar in a small saucepan with 100ml (3½fl oz) of water and bring to the boil, allowing the syrup to reduce by about half.
6. When the cake is cooked, pour the syrup over it while it is still hot, allowing it to soak into the sponge. Leave the loaf to cool a little before turning it out of the tin on to a wire rack to cool down fully before serving.

VANILLA CUPCAKES

An old favourite, these are the cupcakes that fly off our bakery shelves every day! If you want to convert the recipe into a single three-layer cake, double the quantities for the sponge and frosting, and bake the batter in three 20cm (8in) sandwich tins.

Makes 12–16 cupcakes

FOR THE SPONGE
80g (3oz) unsalted butter, softened
280g (10oz) caster sugar
240g (8½oz) plain flour
1 tbsp baking powder
¼ tsp salt
240ml (8½fl oz) whole milk
½ tsp vanilla essence
2 large eggs

FOR THE VANILLA FROSTING
500g (1lb 2oz) icing sugar
160g (5½oz) unsalted butter, softened
50ml (1¾fl oz) whole milk
½ tsp vanilla essence
Food colouring (optional)
Sprinkles, nuts (such as walnuts or pecans) or sugar-coated mini eggs, to decorate

One or two 12-hole deep muffin tins

1. Preheat the oven to 190°C (375°F), Gas mark 5, and line a muffin tin with muffin cases.

2. Using a hand-held electric whisk or a freestanding electric mixer with the paddle attachment, slowly beat together the butter, sugar, flour, baking powder and salt until the ingredients are well mixed in and resemble fine breadcrumbs.

3. Mix together the milk, vanilla essence and eggs by hand in a jug. With the whisk or mixer still on a low speed, pour three-quarters of the milk mixture into the dry ingredients and mix well, scraping down the sides of the bowl to make sure all the ingredients are fully incorporated. Add the rest of the milk mixture and beat again, now on a medium speed, until the batter is smooth.

4. Spoon the batter into the muffin cases, up to about two-thirds full. If there is any batter left over, it can be used to fill up to four more cases in a second muffin tin. Pop in the oven and bake for 18–20 minutes or until the sponges feel springy when you touch them. Leave to cool slightly before removing from the tin and placing on a wire rack to cool completely.

5. To make the frosting, whisk the icing sugar with the butter on a low speed using the electric whisk, or in the freestanding mixer with the paddle attachment, until fully combined and sandy in consistency. Add the vanilla essence to the milk and pour into the butter and icing sugar while still mixing on a low speed, then increase the speed to high and whisk the frosting until light and fluffy.

6. If you wish to colour the frosting as shown in the photograph, divide it into separate bowls and add a few drops of your chosen food colouring to each bowl, mixing with the frosting until you reach the desired depth of colour. Be careful not to add too much colouring or it won't taste nice.

7. Once the cupcakes are cool, add the frosting, smoothing and swirling with a palette knife, and decorate with coloured or chocolate sprinkles, chopped nuts or sugar-coated mini eggs for Easter.

VARIATION
Vanilla cupcakes with chocolate frosting: Follow the above recipe, but top with the same quantity of chocolate frosting, instead of the vanilla frosting (see Chocolate Cupcakes on page 126).

COURGETTE, WALNUT AND CINNAMON LAYER CAKE

We love putting courgettes in our sweet recipes; they add great moisture and colour to the sponge. Greek yoghurt gives this frosting a tangy, creamy taste.

Serves 10–12

FOR THE SPONGE

3 large eggs
300ml (10½fl oz) sunflower oil
300g (10½oz) soft light
   brown sugar
½ tsp vanilla essence
300g (10½oz) plain flour
1 tsp baking powder
1 tsp bicarbonate of soda
2 tsp ground cinnamon
½ tsp ground ginger
½ tsp ground nutmeg
300g (10½oz) peeled and
   grated courgettes
100g (3½oz) walnuts, roughly
   chopped, plus 10–12 extra
   halves (caramelised if you wish,
   see page 248) to decorate

FOR THE FROSTING

240g (8½oz) unsalted butter,
   softened
1½ tsp ground cinnamon,
   plus extra for dusting
750g (1lb 10oz) icing sugar
75g (2½oz) plain Greek yoghurt

*Three 20cm (8in) diameter
loose-bottomed sandwich tins*

1. Preheat the oven to 170°C (325°F), Gas mark 3, and line the bases of the sandwich tins with baking parchment.

2. Using a hand-held electric whisk or a freestanding electric mixer with the paddle attachment, mix together the eggs, sunflower oil, sugar and vanilla essence until they are all combined.

3. Sift together the flour, baking powder, bicarbonate of soda and the ground spices. With the mixer or electric whisk running on a low speed, add these to the eggs, sugar and sunflower oil in two batches, beating well after each addition until all the ingredients are incorporated. Lastly, add the courgettes and chopped walnuts to the batter, mixing them in thoroughly.

4. Divide the cake batter evenly between the three prepared cake tins and bake for 35–40 minutes or until golden on top and springy to the touch. Allow the cakes to cool in the tins for a few minutes before carefully turning them out on to a wire rack to cool completely.

5. While the cakes are cooling, make the frosting. Mix together the butter, cinnamon and icing sugar using the electric whisk or freestanding mixer with the paddle attachment. Keep mixing until the butter is fully incorporated and the mixture is sandy in consistency.

6. Add the yoghurt and mix on a low speed until the ingredients are combined, then increase the speed and beat until the frosting is light and fluffy.

7. Once the cake layers have fully cooled, place the first layer of sponge on a plate or cake card and top with 3–4 tablespoons of the frosting, smoothing it out using a palette knife and adding a little more if needed. Sandwich the second layer of cake on top and add another 3–4 tablespoons of the frosting, then add the final layer and use the remaining frosting to cover the top and sides of the cake.

8. To finish, you can make a swirled pattern in the frosting using the tip of your palette knife. Dust with a little ground cinnamon and decorate with walnut halves, caramelised if you wish (see page 248).

MARBLED CUPCAKES

Now you don't have to decide whether to make chocolate or vanilla cupcakes ... you can make them both at once! For Easter, you could decorate each cake with contrasting milk and white chocolate mini eggs.

Makes 12–16 cupcakes

**FOR THE CHOCOLATE
AND VANILLA SPONGES**
80g (3oz) unsalted butter,
  softened
280g (10oz) caster sugar
240g (8½oz) plain flour
1 tbsp baking powder
½ tsp salt
20g (¾oz) cocoa powder
2 large eggs
240ml (8½fl oz) whole milk
½ tsp vanilla essence

FOR THE CHOCOLATE FROSTING
200g (7oz) icing sugar
50g (1¾oz) cocoa powder
80g (3oz) unsalted butter,
  softened
25ml (1fl oz) whole milk

FOR THE VANILLA FROSTING
250g (9oz) icing sugar
80g (3oz) unsalted butter,
  softened
25ml (1fl oz) whole milk
¼ tsp vanilla essence

*One or two 12-hole
deep muffin tins*

1. Preheat the oven to 190°C (375°F), Gas mark 5, and line a muffin tin with muffin cases.
2. First make the flavoured sponges, beginning with the chocolate one. Using a hand-held electric whisk or a freestanding electric mixer with the paddle attachment, beat together half each of the butter, sugar, flour, baking powder and salt, along with all of the cocoa powder, on a low speed until resembling fine breadcrumbs.
3. Whisk the eggs with the milk by hand in a jug, then pour half of this mixture into a second jug and set aside for the vanilla sponge.
4. Take the first jug with the egg mixture, pour three-quarters of it into the dry chocolate sponge ingredients and mix on a low speed to combine. Adjust the speed to medium and continue mixing until smooth and thick. Scrape down the sides of the bowl, then add the remaining quarter of egg mixture from the first jug and continue to mix on a medium speed until all the ingredients are incorporated and the batter is smooth once again.
5. For the vanilla sponge, repeat step 2 with the remaining half of the butter, sugar, flour, baking powder and salt, but this time no cocoa powder. Take the second jug of egg mixture, whisk in the vanilla essence, then repeat step 4, pouring it into the dry vanilla sponge ingredients and mixing as described.
6. Divide the chocolate batter between the muffin cases, filling each by about a third. Top with the same quantity of vanilla batter and use a teaspoon handle to swirl the two mixtures together. If any batter remains, use it to fill more cases in a separate muffin tin.
7. Place in the oven and bake for 18–20 minutes or until well risen and springy to the touch. Let the cupcakes cool in the tin for a few minutes, then transfer to a wire rack and leave to cool completely before you frost them.
8. To make the chocolate frosting, whisk the icing sugar with the cocoa powder and butter on a low speed in the freestanding mixer with the paddle attachment, or using the electric whisk, until the mixture is sandy in consistency. Pour in the milk, still mixing on a low speed, then increase the speed to high and whisk the frosting until soft and fluffy.
9. Repeat this step for the vanilla frosting, but omitting the cocoa powder and mixing the vanilla essence with the milk before adding it to the frosting.
10. When the cupcakes have cooled, spread 1 tablespoon of each frosting on to each cake using a palette knife, then swirl the two for a marbled effect.

SUMMER AFTERNOON TEA

SUMMER FRUIT CHEESECAKE

Make sure you don't overcook cheesecakes; they are ready when slightly golden and still have a bit of wobble in the middle! The lovely summer berries dotted throughout this cake burst with flavour.

Serves 8–12

FOR THE BISCUIT BASE
220g (8oz) digestive biscuits
100g (3½oz) unsalted butter, melted

FOR THE CHEESECAKE TOPPING
700g (1½lb) full-fat cream cheese (such as Philadelphia)
1 tsp vanilla essence
120g (4oz) caster sugar
3 large eggs
80g (3oz) frozen summer fruits or mixed berries (defrosted), plus extra berries to decorate (optional)
Whipped soured cream, to serve (optional)

One 20cm (8in) diameter spring-form cake tin

1. First line the base of the cake tin with baking parchment. Place the biscuits in a food processor and whiz into fine crumbs using the blade attachment. If you prefer, place the biscuits in a plastic bag, seal it closed and crush with a rolling pin.
2. Tip the biscuit crumbs into a bowl, add the melted butter and mix together with a spoon, then place the mixture in the prepared tin, pressing it into the base with the back of the spoon. Place in the fridge to cool and set for 20–30 minutes.
3. Meanwhile, preheat the oven to 160°C (320°F), Gas mark 3, and make the cheesecake topping.
4. Using a hand-held electric whisk or a freestanding electric mixer with the paddle attachment, mix together the cream cheese, vanilla essence and sugar on a medium speed until smooth. Break the eggs in one at a time, mixing thoroughly after each addition and scraping down the sides of the bowl to make sure every bit is incorporated. Stir in the summer fruits by hand, checking they are evenly dispersed, then pour the mixture into the prepared tin.
5. Wrap the tin in foil (see the tip on page 80), place in a roasting tin and fill this with water to about 5mm (¼in) from the top of the cake tin, creating a water bath (or bain marie) for the cheesecake to bake in. The moisture created in the oven helps to prevent the top of the cheesecake from cracking. Run a palette knife around the inside edge of the tin; this releases the mixture from the sides so that it doesn't stick.
6. Place in the oven and bake for 35–45 minutes or until the cheesecake is a light-golden colour on top (more so around the edges) and generally firm to the touch, with only a slight wobble in the middle.
7. Keeping the cheesecake in the tin, allow it to cool down at room temperature, then place in the fridge to set for a few hours, or preferably overnight. Once the cheesecake has set, it can be taken out of the tin and decorated with extra berries (fresh ones, if you prefer) or whipped soured cream.

EARL GREY TEA CUPCAKES

We created these cupcakes as part of our hot drinks range. Earl Grey tea has a lovely bergamot flavour that gives these cupcakes a subtle edge. Variations can be made using herbal and fruit teas (see below).

Makes 12–16 cupcakes

FOR THE SPONGE
3 Earl Grey teabags
3 tbsp just-boiled water
80g (3oz) unsalted butter, softened
280g (10oz) caster sugar
240g (8½oz) plain flour
1 tbsp baking powder
¼ tsp salt
200ml (7fl oz) whole milk
2 large eggs

FOR THE FROSTING
50ml (1¾fl oz) whole milk
500g (1lb 2oz) icing sugar
160g (5½oz) unsalted butter, softened

One or two 12-hole deep muffin tins

1. Place the teabags in a bowl and add the just-boiled water, then leave to brew for 30 minutes.
2. Preheat the oven to 190°C (375°F), Gas mark 5, and line a muffin tin with muffin cases. Use a hand-held electric whisk or freestanding electric mixer with paddle attachment to mix the butter, sugar, flour, baking powder and salt on a low speed until the texture of fine breadcrumbs.
3. Pour the milk into a jug, add the eggs and whisk by hand. Add the brewed tea, squeezing every last drop from the teabags into the milk mixture, then set the teabags aside for the frosting.
4. Pour three-quarters of the milk mixture into the dry ingredients and mix on a low speed to combine. Then mix on a medium speed until smooth and thick. Scrape the sides of the bowl, add the remaining milk mixture and beat until all the ingredients have come together and the batter is smooth.
5. Divide the batter between the paper cases, filling each two-thirds full. If there is batter left over, spoon it into more cases in a separate tin. Bake in the oven for 18–20 minutes or until risen and springy to the touch, then leave to cool slightly in the tin before transferring to a wire rack to cool fully.
6. While the cupcakes are cooking, place the used teabags in a small bowl with the milk for the frosting and leave to infuse for 30 minutes. Remove the teabags and give them a good squeeze to extract maximum flavour.
7. Using the electric whisk or freestanding mixer with paddle attachment, whisk the icing sugar with the butter on a low speed until no large lumps of butter remain and the mixture is still powdery. Pour in the tea-infused milk while mixing slowly, then increase the speed to high and whisk until soft and fluffy.
8. Divide the frosting between the cold cupcakes, smoothing the tops and swirling with a palette knife.

VARIATIONS

Peppermint tea cupcakes: Make as above but use 3 peppermint teabags instead of Earl Grey.

Fruit tea cupcakes: Make as above but with 3 fruit teabags of your choice, such as summer fruits, mixed berry, strawberry or raspberry, and top the frosted cupcakes with fruit to match, such as summer berries or slices of fresh strawberry.

ORANGE, ALMOND AND YOGHURT LOAF

This simple and quick-to-make loaf is a lovely afternoon treat. Putting yoghurt in the sponge keeps it moist and rich, and the orange zest livens things up.

Serves 8–10

190g (7oz) unsalted butter,
  plus extra for greasing
190g (7oz) plain flour,
  plus extra for dusting
1 tbsp finely grated orange zest
190g (7oz) caster sugar
3 large eggs
60g (2oz) ground almonds
1 tsp baking powder
¼ tsp salt
25g (1oz) plain yoghurt
1 tsp vanilla essence
10g (⅓oz) flaked almonds

One 8.5 x 17.5cm (3½ x 7in)
loaf tin with 7.5cm (3in) sides

1. Preheat the oven to 170°C (325°F), Gas mark 3, then grease the loaf tin with butter and dust with flour.
2. Using a hand-held electric whisk or a freestanding electric mixer with the paddle attachment, cream together the butter, orange zest and sugar until the mixture is soft and fluffy. Add the eggs one at a time, whisking well after each addition. Scrape down the sides of the bowl every now and then to ensure the eggs and butter are properly mixed in.
3. In a separate bowl, mix together the flour, ground almonds, baking powder and salt. Tip the dry ingredients into the creamed mixture in two batches and whisk together on a low speed until just incorporated, then mix in the yoghurt and vanilla essence.
4. Pour the batter into the prepared loaf tin and sprinkle the flaked almonds on top. Place in the oven and bake for 50–60 minutes or until the sponge is firm on top and a skewer inserted into the centre of the cake comes out clean. Remove from the oven and allow the loaf to cool a little before turning it out of the tin on to a wire rack to cool completely for serving.

LEMON MERINGUE CUPCAKES

One of our favourites! Slices of lemon meringue pie fly off the shelves at our bakeries, so we thought we'd make a cupcake version to please our readers.

Makes 12–16 cupcakes

FOR THE SPONGE

80g (3oz) unsalted butter, softened
280g (10oz) caster sugar
240g (8½oz) plain flour
1 tbsp baking powder
¼ tsp salt
1 tsp finely grated lemon zest
2 large eggs
240ml (8½fl oz) whole milk

FOR THE FILLING AND FROSTING

200g (7oz) caster sugar
4 egg whites
70g (2½oz) lemon curd

One or two 12-hole deep muffin tins
Cook's blowtorch (optional)

1. Preheat the oven to 190°C (375°F), Gas mark 5, and line a muffin tin with muffin cases.
2. Using a hand-held electric whisk or a freestanding electric mixer with the paddle attachment, beat together the butter, sugar, flour, baking powder, salt and lemon zest on a low speed until the ingredients are well incorporated and resemble fine breadcrumbs.
3. Break the eggs into a jug, add the milk and whisk together by hand. Pour three-quarters of the milk and eggs into the dry ingredients and mix on a low speed to combine. Increase the speed to medium and keep beating until smooth and thick, scraping down the sides of the bowl from time to time. Pour in the remaining milk and eggs and continue to mix on a medium speed until all the ingredients are incorporated and the batter is smooth.
4. Spoon the batter into the paper cases, filling each by about two-thirds. If any batter is left over, use it to fill up to four more cases in a second tin. Bake in the oven for 18–20 minutes or until risen and springy to the touch. Leave to cool slightly before removing from the tin and placing on a wire rack. The cakes will need to cool completely before you frost them.
5. To make the frosting, put the sugar into a small saucepan, cover with water (about 150ml/5½fl oz) and bring to the boil. Meanwhile, using the electric whisk or freestanding mixer with the paddle attachment, whisk the egg whites until just foamy.
6. Allow the sugar to boil for 5–10 minutes or until it has reached the soft-ball stage (see the tip overleaf), then increase the mixer speed to medium and pour the sugar on to the egg whites. (Be very careful as the sugar is extremely hot and will burn if it comes into contact with your skin.) When all the sugar has been added, increase the speed to high and whisk until the underside of the bowl feels lukewarm. The meringue should have quadrupled in size and be very white, smooth and fairly shiny.

Continues overleaf >

7. Once the cupcakes have fully cooled, lay them out on a tray and hollow out the middle of each cake using a sharp knife. Make the hole about 2cm (¾in) deep and 2cm (¾in) wide and keep each cut-out piece of sponge. Using a teaspoon, fill the holes about half full with the lemon curd and place the cut-out piece of sponge back on top, trimming to fit if needed.

8. Top the cupcakes with the prepared meringue, using a tablespoon and swirling the frosting to resemble the top of a lemon meringue pie. Using a cook's blowtorch, lightly brown the meringue to give it a baked appearance. If you don't have a blowtorch, simply pop the frosted cupcakes under a hot grill for a few seconds to brown them. (The meringue will brown very quickly, so keep a close eye on them so that they don't burn.)

TIP

To check whether your sugar syrup has reached the soft-ball stage, use a spoon to drop a small amount into a bowl of very cold water. If the syrup has been cooked to the correct heat, it will form a soft ball in the water. Removed from the cold water, this ball won't retain its shape but will flatten in your hand.

BLUEBERRY AND
SOURED CREAM LOAF

A classic American cake that is easy to bake and keeps well in a sealed tin. Please don't worry if your blueberries sink during baking, that's perfectly normal. You can substitute other small berries if you prefer.

Serves 8–10

190g (7oz) unsalted butter,
  softened, plus extra
  for greasing
190g (7oz) plain flour,
  plus extra for dusting
190g (7oz) caster sugar
3 eggs
1 tsp baking powder
¼ tsp salt
25ml (1fl oz) soured cream
120g (4oz) fresh or frozen
  (and defrosted) blueberries

*One 8.5 x 17.5cm (3½ x 7in)
loaf tin with 7.5cm (3in) sides*

1. Preheat the oven to 170°C (325°F), Gas mark 3, then grease the loaf tin with butter and dust with flour.
2. Using a hand-held electric whisk or a freestanding electric mixer with the paddle attachment, cream together the butter and sugar until pale and fluffy. Break the eggs in one at a time, whisking well after each addition and scraping down the sides of the bowl to make sure all the ingredients are mixed together thoroughly.
3. Sift together the flour, baking powder and salt, then tip into the creamed butter and eggs in two batches and lightly mix until just incorporated. Add the soured cream, then stir the blueberries into the batter by hand, making sure the berries are evenly distributed throughout the mixture.
4. Pour or spoon the batter into the prepared loaf tin, then bake in the oven for 50–60 minutes or until the sponge is firm and a skewer inserted into the middle of the loaf comes out with no cake batter sticking to it. Allow the loaf to cool for a while in the tin before turning it out on to a wire rack to cool down completely.

PLUM CUPCAKES

A delicious summer cupcake, the buttermilk and plum jam make the sponge really moist. Decorate with slices of ripe plum; you can also dust with sugar if you like.

Makes 12–16 cupcakes

FOR THE SPONGE

120g (4oz) unsalted butter, softened
340g (12oz) plain flour
½ tsp baking powder
½ tsp salt
4 large egg yolks
360g (12½oz) soft light brown sugar
180ml (6½fl oz) buttermilk
270g (10oz) plum jam

FOR THE FROSTING

500g (1lb 2oz) icing sugar
160g (5½oz) unsalted butter, softened
50ml (1¾fl oz) whole milk
70g (2½oz) plum jam
Fresh plum slices, to decorate

One or two 12-hole deep muffin tins

1. Preheat the oven to 190°C (375°F), Gas mark 5, and line a muffin tin with muffin cases.
2. Using a hand-held electric whisk or a freestanding electric mixer with the paddle attachment, mix together the butter, flour, baking powder and salt on a low speed until the ingredients are well incorporated and crumb-like in texture.
3. In a jug and using a hand whisk, mix together the egg yolks, brown sugar, buttermilk and 120g (4oz) of the jam until all the ingredients are combined. Add half of this mixture to the dry ingredients and mix on a low speed until combined. Continue to add the remaining mixture, then increase the speed to medium and mix until smooth.
4. Fill each paper case up to one-third full with batter, then top with 1 teaspoon of the remaining plum jam, followed by a similar quantity of batter (filling each case up to about two-thirds full). The jam will create a filling as the cakes bake. If any batter and jam remain, use them to fill one to four more paper cases in a separate tin.
5. Bake for approximately 20 minutes or until the tops of the cupcakes spring back when you lightly press them. Leave to cool slightly before removing from the tin and transferring to a wire rack to cool completely while you make the frosting.
6. Using either the electric whisk or freestanding mixer with the paddle attachment, whisk the icing sugar with the butter on a low speed until fully incorporated and still powdery in consistency. Pour in the milk while mixing on a low speed, then increase the speed to high and whisk until soft and fluffy. Finally, stir in the plum jam by hand, ensuring it is evenly dispersed.
7. Spoon the frosting on to the cupcakes once they are cold, gently smoothing the tops with a palette knife and adding a decorative swirl, if you wish. Decorate with slices of fresh plum.

LEMONADE CUPCAKES

Our soda range of cupcakes was a big hit with our customers. These fresh-tasting lemonade cakes include popping candy in the frosting when made in our bakeries, but at home it's easier to use fizzy lemon jelly sweets, if you wish. See the variation below for the fizzy orange cupcakes shown in the photograph.

Makes 12–16 cupcakes

FOR THE SPONGE
80g (3oz) unsalted butter, softened
280g (10oz) caster sugar
240g (8½oz) plain flour
1 tbsp baking powder
¼ tsp salt
½ tsp finely grated lemon zest
1 tbsp lemonade syrup
240ml (8½fl oz) whole milk
2 large eggs

FOR THE FROSTING
2 tbsp lemonade syrup
50ml (1¾fl oz) whole milk
500g (1lb 2oz) icing sugar
160g (5½oz) unsalted butter, softened
1 tsp finely grated lemon zest
Lemon jelly sweets or lemon slices, to decorate (optional)

One or two 12-hole deep muffin tins

1. Preheat the oven to 190°C (375°F), Gas mark 5, and line a muffin tin with muffin cases.
2. Using a hand-held electric whisk or a freestanding electric mixer with the paddle attachment, set on a low speed, beat together the butter, sugar, flour, baking powder, salt and lemon zest until all the ingredients have come together and resemble fine breadcrumbs.
3. Mix the lemonade syrup with the milk in a jug, add the eggs and whisk together by hand, then pour three-quarters of this milk mixture into the dry ingredients and mix on a low speed to combine. Increase the speed to medium and keep mixing the batter until thick and smooth. Scrape down the sides of the bowl, add the remaining milk mixture and continue to beat on a medium speed until all the ingredients are incorporated and the batter is smooth once again.
4. Spoon the batter into the paper cases, filling each case by about two-thirds. Any remaining batter can be used to fill one to four more cases in a second muffin tin. Pop in the oven and bake for 18–20 minutes or until risen and springy to the touch. Leave to cool slightly before removing from the tin, then place on a wire rack to cool completely before you add the frosting.
5. To make the frosting, first mix the lemonade syrup with the milk. Using the electric whisk or freestanding mixer with the paddle attachment, whisk the icing sugar with the butter and lemon zest on a low speed until sandy in texture. Mixing on a low speed, pour the flavoured milk into the icing sugar and butter mixture. When you've poured it all in, increase the speed to high and whisk until light and fluffy.
6. Spoon a generous dollop of frosting on to each cold cupcake, then gently smooth over with a palette knife, making a swirl at the top and adding lemon jelly sweets or lemon slices, if you wish.

VARIATION
Fizzy orange cupcakes: Bake and frost the cupcakes exactly as in the recipe above, but use fizzy orange syrup and orange zest instead of lemon, in both the cake mixture and the frosting. If you'd like to decorate the cakes once they've been frosted, use orange jelly sweets or orange slices.

PEACH AND RASPBERRY TART

The perfect dessert for a summery meal, this beautiful tart is topped with fresh fruits, so is best eaten straightaway.

Serves 8–10

FOR THE PASTRY
110g (4oz) unsalted butter,
    softened
225g (8oz) plain flour,
    plus extra for dusting
80g (3oz) caster sugar
1 large egg

FOR THE FILLING
500ml (18fl oz) whole milk
¼ tsp vanilla essence
5 egg yolks
200g (7oz) caster sugar
20g (¾oz) plain flour
20g (¾oz) cornflour
150ml (5½fl oz) double cream

FOR THE TOPPING
4 peaches, peeled and sliced
    and stones removed
100g (3½oz) fresh or frozen
    (and defrosted) raspberries
30g (1oz) caster sugar,
    for sprinkling
Handful of fresh mint leaves

*One 23cm (9in) diameter
loose-bottomed tart tin*

1. Using a freestanding electric mixer with the paddle attachment, mix the butter and flour on a low speed until it has a crumb-like consistency. Add the sugar, then the egg, mixing gently to incorporate. Alternatively, rub the butter and flour with your fingertips, then stir in the sugar and egg. When a dough forms, remove from the bowl and knead gently on a floured work surface to bring it together. Cover in cling film and place in the fridge to rest for 20–30 minutes.

2. Once rested, roll out the pastry on a lightly floured surface to about 5mm (¼in) thick, and large enough to fit your tart tin. Gently press the pastry down into the base and sides of the tin and cut away any overhang. Prick the base several times and put the tart case in the fridge to rest for 20–30 minutes.

3. Preheat the oven to 170°C (325°F), Gas mark 3. Once the tart base has rested, line with baking parchment and fill with baking beans, then place in the oven and bake 'blind' for 12 minutes. Carefully remove the beans and paper and bake the pastry for another 15 minutes or until cooked through and lightly golden in colour. Set aside to cool.

4. While the pastry is baking, make the filling. Bring the milk and vanilla essence to the boil in a saucepan. In a bowl, mix together the egg yolks, sugar, flour and cornflour to a thick paste. If it is too dry to come together, add 1 tablespoon of the hot milk to loosen it up.

5. When the milk has come to the boil, remove from the heat and add 4–5 tablespoons to the bowl of paste, stirring until the paste becomes a thick liquid. Pour this into the pan of milk and set over a low heat. Stirring constantly, bring to the boil and allow to thicken – boil for at least 1 minute to fully cook the flour. Pour this custard on to a baking tray to cool, covering straight away with cling film so that it doesn't develop a skin. Allow the custard to cool completely for 30–40 minutes.

6. Whip the double cream, either by hand or using a hand-held electric whisk, until soft peaks form. Scrape the cooled custard into another bowl, stirring to break it up and until the texture is completely smooth. Fold the whipped cream into the custard, then pour into the cooked tart case and place in the fridge to set for 1–2 hours.

7. When the custard cream has set, arrange the sliced peaches and raspberries on top, sprinkle with sugar and scatter with mint leaves. Once the fruit has been added, the pie is best eaten straight away.

RASPBERRY TRIFLE CUPCAKE

This cupcake really does taste like the best trifle you've ever eaten! You can try it with other fruits if you prefer, but we love the classic raspberry, cream and vanilla sponge combination.

Makes 12–16 cupcakes

FOR THE SPONGE
80g (3oz) unsalted butter, softened
280g (10oz) caster sugar
240g (8½oz) plain flour
1 tbsp baking powder
¼ tsp salt
240ml (8½fl oz) whole milk
1 tsp vanilla essence
2 large eggs

FOR THE FILLING AND FROSTING
500ml (18fl oz) whole milk
½ tsp vanilla essence
5 egg yolks
100g (3½oz) caster sugar
30g (1oz) plain flour
30g (1oz) cornflour
200ml (7fl oz) double cream
24–32 fresh raspberries
100g (3½oz) raspberry jam

One or two 12-hole deep muffin tins
Piping bag (optional)

1. Preheat the oven to 190°C (375°F), Gas mark 5, and line a muffin tin with muffin cases.
2. Using a hand-held electric whisk or a freestanding electric mixer with the paddle attachment, beat together the butter, sugar, flour, baking powder and salt on a slow speed until the ingredients are well mixed and resemble fine breadcrumbs.
3. In a jug whisk together the milk, vanilla essence and eggs by hand, then pour three-quarters of this into the dry ingredients, while mixing on a slow speed, and beat together, scraping down the sides of the bowl to make sure all the ingredients are well incorporated. Add the remaining milk mixture and beat again, on a medium speed, until the batter is smooth.
4. Divide the batter between the muffin cases, filling each one two-thirds full. Any remaining batter can be used to fill up to four more cases in an additional tin. Bake the cupcakes for 18–20 minutes or until the sponges bounce back when lightly pressed. Leave to cool slightly before removing from the tin and placing on a wire rack to cool down fully.
5. While the cupcakes are cooking, make the custard for the filling and topping. Place the milk in a saucepan with the vanilla essence and bring to the boil. In a bowl mix together the egg yolks, sugar, flour and cornflour to make a paste, adding 1 tablespoon of the hot milk to thin it if necessary.
6. When the milk has boiled, remove the pan from the heat and mix 4–5 tablespoons with the egg and flour paste, then pour this back into the pan with the remaining hot milk and return to the heat. Bring back up to the boil, whisking constantly, and continue to boil for a further minute to ensure the flour and cornflour are fully cooked. Pour the custard into a baking tray, cover with cling film and set aside to cool for 30–40 minutes.

Continues overleaf >

7. Tip the cooled custard into a large bowl and beat with a wooden spoon to break up any lumps. In a separate bowl whip the double cream into soft peaks, either by hand or using the electric whisk. Fold the whipped cream into the custard and use to fill a piping bag (if using).

8. Using a sharp knife, make a hollow in the centre of each cupcake – approximately 2cm (¾in) in diameter and 3cm (1¼in) deep – retaining the cut-out pieces of sponge. Place a raspberry upside down in the hollow of each cake, then spoon ½ teaspoon of jam on top, followed by the same amount of custard, either piped or spooned into the hollow.

9. Replace the cut-out pieces of sponge, trimming to fit and pressing down gently to ensure that the top is level with the rest of the cake, then pipe or spoon the custard topping in a circular motion (like whippy ice cream) on top of each cake. Add a fresh raspberry on top of the swirled custard to finish.

STRAWBERRIES AND CREAM CHEESECAKE

The classic summer pairing of strawberries and cream never fails to delight. This thick and creamy cheesecake should be decorated with strawberry slices at the last minute, so that the slices don't bleed too much colour into the cream topping.

Serves 8–12

FOR THE BASE
220g (8oz) digestive biscuits
100g (3½oz) unsalted butter, melted

FOR THE TOPPING
200g (7oz) fresh strawberries, hulled and chopped, plus 100–200g (3½–7oz) extra strawberries, cut in half, to decorate
180g (6½oz) caster sugar
600g (1lb 5oz) full-fat cream cheese (such as Philadelphia)
2 large eggs
100g (3½oz) mascarpone cheese
20g (¾oz) icing sugar
100ml (3½fl oz) double cream

One 20cm (8in) diameter spring-form cake tin

1. Line the base of the tin with baking parchment. Using a food processor with the blade attachment, blitz the biscuits into fine crumbs. Alternatively, place them in a plastic bag, seal and crush with a rolling pin.
2. Pour the biscuit crumbs into a bowl, add the melted butter and stir together, then tip into the lined tin and press into the base with the back of a spoon. Place the tin in the fridge for 20–30 minutes to allow the base to set.
3. Meanwhile, place the strawberries in a saucepan with 80g (3oz) of the sugar and 30ml (1fl oz) of water and bring to the boil. Reduce the heat and cook until the strawberries are soft and the liquid has reduced by half. Take off the hob and set aside until completely cold.
4. Preheat the oven to 160°C (320°F), Gas mark 3. Prepare the topping by using a hand-held electric whisk or a freestanding electric mixer with the paddle attachment to beat together the cream cheese and remaining sugar on a medium speed until smooth. Add the eggs one at a time, mixing well after each addition and scraping the sides of the bowl now and then. Tip in the cooked strawberries and stir in by hand, ensuring that they are evenly dispersed.
5. Pour the mixture into the prepared tin – it should be about two-thirds full. Place in a roasting tin (first wrap the cake tin in foil – see tip on page 80) and fill this with water up to about 5mm (¼in) from the top of the cake tin. This creates a water bath in which to bake the cheesecake, preventing it from drying out and cracking in the oven.
6. Bake for approximately 30 minutes or until firm on top with a very slight wobble in the centre. Allow the cheesecake to cool to room temperature still in the tin, then place in the fridge to chill and set for 1–2 hours.
7. Using the electric whisk or freestanding mixer, beat the mascarpone and icing sugar on a medium speed until smooth. In a separate bowl, whip the double cream until soft peaks form, then fold it into the mascarpone.
8. Remove the chilled cheesecake from the fridge and pour the mascarpone cream on top, spreading it evenly. Place back in the fridge for a few hours, or preferably overnight, to set.
9. When you are ready to serve, carefully remove the cheesecake from the tin and top with fresh strawberry halves.

PEA, HAM AND FETA CHEESE MUFFINS

Perfect served slightly warm for a breakfast or snack on the go.

Makes 10–12 muffins

300g (10½oz) plain flour
1 tbsp baking powder
½ tsp bicarbonate of soda
⅛ tsp salt
2 large eggs
250ml (9fl oz) whole milk
85g (3oz) butter, melted
40g (1½oz) tinned or frozen
   (and defrosted) peas
60g (2oz) sliced, cooked ham,
   cut into small squares
40g (1½oz) feta cheese

One 12-hole deep muffin tin

1. Preheat the oven to 190°C (375°F), Gas mark 5, and line the tin with muffin cases.
2. First sift together the flour, baking powder, bicarbonate of soda and salt into a large bowl or the bowl of a freestanding electric mixer. Break the eggs into a jug, add the milk and mix together.
3. Make a well in the centre of the dry ingredients and pour in the milk and eggs while mixing on a low speed, using either the mixer with the paddle attachment or a hand-held electric whisk. When all of the ingredients have come together, add the melted butter. Scrape down the sides of the bowl, and then mix on a medium speed until the batter is smooth.
4. Add the peas and ham to the mixture and crumble in the feta cheese, then stir these in by hand, making sure they are evenly dispersed throughout the batter.
5. Spoon the batter into the muffin cases, filling them two-thirds full, and bake for 25–30 minutes or until the tops of the muffins are nicely golden and springy to the touch. Allow to cool in the tin for a few minutes and then transfer to a wire rack.

BIRTHDAYS & CELEBRATIONS

CHOCOLATE CUPCAKES

Another one of our ever-popular Hummingbird staples, our chocolate cupcakes have pleased our customers since 2004. If you want to convert the recipe into a single three-layer chocolate cake, then simply double the sponge and frosting quantities, and bake the batter in three 20cm (8in) sandwich tins.

Makes 12–16 cupcakes

FOR THE SPONGE
80g (3oz) unsalted butter, softened
280g (10oz) caster sugar
200g (7oz) plain flour
40g (1½oz) cocoa powder
1 tbsp baking powder
¼ tsp salt
240ml (8½fl oz) whole milk
2 large eggs

FOR THE FROSTING
400g (14oz) icing sugar
100g (3½oz) cocoa powder
160g (5½oz) unsalted butter, softened
50ml (1¾fl oz) whole milk
Chocolate or coloured sprinkles, chocolate shavings or chopped nuts, to decorate (optional)

One or two 12-hole deep muffin tins

1. Preheat the oven to 190°C (375°F), Gas mark 5, and line a muffin tin with muffin cases.
2. Using a hand-held electric whisk or a freestanding electric mixer with the paddle attachment, beat together the butter, sugar, flour, cocoa powder, baking powder and salt on a low speed until the ingredients are well incorporated and resemble fine breadcrumbs.
3. Pour the milk into a jug, add the eggs and whisk together. Pour three-quarters of this mixture into the dry ingredients and beat on a low speed to combine. Raise the speed to medium and continue to mix until smooth and thick, scraping down the sides of the bowl every now and then. Pour in the remaining milk mixture and keep mixing on a medium speed until all the ingredients have come together and the batter is smooth once again.
4. Spoon the batter into the paper cases, so that each is two-thirds full. If any batter remains, use it to fill one to four more cases in a separate tin. Put in the oven and bake for 18–20 minutes or until risen and springy to the touch. Leave to cool slightly before removing from the tin and placing on a wire rack to cool completely before frosting.
5. To make the chocolate frosting, whisk the icing sugar with the cocoa powder and butter on a low speed in the freestanding mixer with the paddle attachment, or using the electric whisk, until the mixture is sandy in consistency. Pour in the milk, still mixing on a low speed, then increase the speed to high and whisk the frosting until soft and fluffy.
6. Once the cupcakes are cool, add the frosting, smoothing and swirling with a palette knife, then decorate, if you want, with sprinkles, chocolate shavings or chopped nuts – anything that takes your fancy.

VARIATION
Chocolate cupcakes with vanilla frosting: Make the cupcakes exactly as above, but instead of the chocolate frosting, cover with the same quantity of vanilla frosting (see Vanilla Cupcakes on page 92).

BANOFFEE WHOOPIE PIES

Banana, cinnamon and *dulce de leche*: three more perfect reasons to make a whoopie pie.

Makes 8–10 pies

FOR THE SPONGE
1 large egg
150g (5½oz) caster sugar
125g (4½oz) plain yoghurt
25ml (1fl oz) milk
¼ tsp vanilla essence
75g (2½oz) unsalted butter,
 melted
275g (10oz) plain flour
¾ tsp bicarbonate of soda
¼ tsp baking powder
½ tsp ground cinnamon
2 bananas

FOR THE FILLING
170g (6oz) unsalted butter,
 softened
280g (10oz) icing sugar
220g (8oz) vanilla
 Marshmallow Fluff
2 tbsp tinned caramel
 or *dulce de leche*

1. Using a hand-held electric whisk or a freestanding electric mixer with the paddle attachment, whisk the egg and sugar until pale and fluffy. Stir together the yoghurt, milk and vanilla essence in a jug, then gradually add this to the egg mixture, beating on a low speed until combined. Add the melted butter and mix again.
2. Sift together the flour, bicarbonate of soda, baking powder and cinnamon, then add these to the liquid ingredients in two batches, mixing well on a low speed after each addition to ensure everything is well combined.
3. Peel the bananas and, using your fingers, break them up into small, rough pieces, then stir into the batter by hand, trying not to over-mix. Put the batter in the fridge and allow to cool and set for 20–30 minutes.
4. Meanwhile, preheat the oven to 170°C (325°F), Gas mark 3, and line two baking trays with baking parchment.
5. Remove the batter from the fridge and spoon on to the prepared trays in 3–5cm (1¼–2in) diameter mounds, making 16–20 in total, each 2–3cm (¾–1¼in) apart. Place in the oven and bake for 10–13 minutes or until lightly golden and springy to the touch. Allow to cool completely on a wire rack before you fill them.
6. While the sponges are cooking, make the filling. Using the electric whisk or freestanding mixer with the paddle attachment, mix together the butter and the icing sugar on a low speed until blended. Add the marshmallow fluff and continue to beat, on a high speed, until light and fluffy. Beat in the caramel and then place in the fridge for 30 minutes to firm up slightly.
7. When the sponges are cold to the touch, spread the flat side of one with 2 tablespoons of the filling and then sandwich together with another sponge (flat side down). Assemble the remaining sponges in the same way.

COCONUT JAM SANDWICH BARS

A coconuty, crunchy take on a jam sandwich. We've used strawberry jam, but of course you can use your favourite jam flavour such as raspberry, blackberry or plum.

Makes 10–12 bars

FOR THE BASE
30g (1oz) unsalted butter
175g (6oz) plain flour
½ tsp baking powder
50g (1¾oz) caster sugar
2 large egg yolks

FOR THE TOPPING
175g (6oz) desiccated coconut
175g (6oz) caster sugar
4 egg whites
50g (1¾oz) plain flour
150g (5½oz) strawberry jam

One 22 x 31cm (9 x 12½in) baking tray

1. Preheat the oven to 170°C (325°F), Gas mark 3, and line the tray with baking parchment.
2. Using a hand-held electric whisk or a freestanding electric mixer with the paddle attachment, slowly mix the butter, flour and baking powder together until the mixture resembles breadcrumbs. Add the sugar and stir in, then tip the egg yolks into a jug and mix with 2 tablespoons of water. Pour the egg mixture into the dry ingredients, and mix until well combined.
3. Press the mixture into the prepared tin, then place in the oven and bake for 12–15 minutes or until the base is a light golden colour. Allow to cool completely before adding the topping – but leave the oven on for cooking the sandwich bars when you've added the topping.
4. In a saucepan, mix together the coconut, sugar and one of the egg whites with 2 tablespoons of water. Stir over a low heat for 3 minutes or until the sugar has dissolved and all the ingredients come together and form a thick paste. Add the flour and continue to cook, stirring constantly, for a further minute. Tip into a large bowl and set aside to cool slightly.
5. Using the electric whisk, whip the remaining 3 egg whites until stiff, then stir one-third into the coconut paste to loosen. Add the remaining whipped egg whites and fold in gently with a large metal spoon until incorporated.
6. Spread the strawberry jam over the cooled base, then top the jam with the coconut mixture, spreading it out evenly. Place in the oven and bake for 25–30 minutes or until the coconut topping is golden brown. Allow the mixture to cool completely in the tin before cutting it into slices.

SWEET AND SALTY CHOCOLATE CAKE

Not as strange as it may sound, this indulgent and utterly delicious cake just has to be tried. Salted caramel is a classic flavour, and mixed into chocolate makes an amazing cake that is well worth the time spent in the kitchen.

Serves 10–12

FOR THE SPONGE
300g (10½oz) unsalted butter, softened
300g (10½oz) caster sugar
140g (5oz) soft light brown sugar
3 eggs
100g (3½oz) cocoa powder
160ml (5½fl oz) buttermilk
1 tsp vanilla essence
330g (11½oz) plain flour
2 tsp baking powder
1 tsp bicarbonate of soda
½ tsp salt

FOR THE SALTY CARAMEL
200g (7oz) caster sugar
2 tbsp golden syrup
120ml (4fl oz) double cream
60ml (2fl oz) soured cream
1 tsp fine sea salt

FOR THE FROSTING
200g (7oz) caster sugar
2 tbsp golden syrup
360ml (12½fl oz) double cream
450g (1lb) dark chocolate (minimum 70% cocoa solids), chopped, plus extra to decorate
450g (1lb) unsalted butter, softened
Sea salt flakes, for sprinkling

Three 20cm (8in) diameter loose-bottomed sandwich tins

1. First make the salty caramel. In a small saucepan bring the sugar and golden syrup to the boil with 60ml (2fl oz) of water, allowing the mixture to boil for about 10 minutes, during which time it should become quite syrupy and a rich caramel colour.

2. Put the double cream, soured cream and salt in a separate pan and bring to the boil, then remove from the heat. The salt should completely dissolve in the cream.

3. When the sugar syrup is ready, remove it from the heat and carefully add the hot cream. It will bubble up as you pour in the cream, but smooth out again quickly after that, becoming a creamier golden colour. Pour the caramel into a small bowl and set it aside to cool while you make the frosting.

4. In a small, clean saucepan, bring the caster sugar and golden syrup to the boil with 60ml (2fl oz) of water, again letting this boil for approximately 10 minutes or until it is syrupy and caramel-coloured.

5. In a separate pan, bring the double cream to the boil. Carefully pour the hot cream into the caramel: as before, it will bubble up, but settle again shortly afterwards. Set this caramel aside to cool slightly.

6. Once it has cooled, add the chopped chocolate, stirring constantly while the chocolate melts. Using a hand-held electric whisk, mix the frosting for about 10 minutes or until the bottom of the bowl feels cool.

7. Add the butter to the chocolate caramel frosting and whisk together until the mixture is light and looks slightly whipped. Place the frosting in the fridge to cool and set for 40–50 minutes while you make the sponge.

8. Preheat the oven to 170°C (325°F), Gas mark 3, and line the bases of the sandwich tins with baking parchment.

9. Using a freestanding electric mixer with the paddle attachment, or a hand-held electric whisk, cream together the butter and both types of sugars until light and fluffy. Add the eggs one at a time, mixing well after each addition and scraping down the sides of the bowl.

Continues overleaf >

10. In a jug stir together the cocoa powder, buttermilk and vanilla essence with 60ml (2fl oz) of water to form a thick paste. Sift together the remaining sponge ingredients, then add these in stages to the creamed butter and sugar, alternating with the cocoa powder paste and mixing thoroughly on a low-to-medium speed until all the ingredients are incorporated.

11. Divide the batter between the three prepared cake tins and bake for approximately 25 minutes or until the top of each sponge feels springy to the touch. Allow the sponges to cool slightly in their tins before turning out on to a wire rack and cooling completely before assembling.

12. Once the sponges feel cold to the touch, place one on a plate or cake card and top with approximately 2 tablespoons of the salty caramel, smoothing it over the sponge using a palette knife. Top the caramel layer with 3–4 tablespoons of the frosting and smooth it out as before.

13. Continue this process, sandwiching together the other two sponges with the remaining salty caramel and a layer of frosting and leaving enough frosting to cover the sides and top of the cake. To finish, decorate the top with chopped chocolate and a light sprinkling of the sea salt flakes.

PEANUT BUTTER AND CHOCOLATE PIE

Peanut butter and chocolate is another delicious American combination that works really well in this easy pie. We use crunchy peanut butter for the added texture, but you can use smooth peanut butter if you prefer.

Serves 8–10

FOR THE BISCUIT BASE
250g (9oz) double-chocolate cookies
175g (6oz) unsalted butter, melted

FOR THE FILLING
3 tbsp cornflour
160g (5½oz) caster sugar
550ml (19½fl oz) whole milk
3 large egg yolks
180g (6½oz) crunchy peanut butter
80g (3oz) dark chocolate (minimum 70% cocoa solids), chopped
250ml (9fl oz) double cream

FOR THE TOPPING
250ml (9fl oz) double cream
50g (1¾oz) icing sugar
50g (1¾oz) unsalted roasted peanuts, roughly chopped

One 22cm (9in) diameter spring-form cake tin with 7cm (3in) sides

1. First line the cake tin with baking parchment, then blitz the cookies to a rough crumb in a food processor with the blade attachment. Pour in the melted butter and blitz again. When both ingredients have come together in a rough paste, remove from the machine and tip into the lined tin.
2. Using the back of a dessertspoon, press the crumb mixture evenly over the base and up the sides of the tin, to a thickness of about 5mm (¼in), then place in the fridge to cool and set for approximately 40 minutes.
3. Meanwhile, make the filling. Mix the cornflour with the sugar in a saucepan, then mix together the milk and egg yolks and pour this into the pan. Place over a low heat and cook until thickened, whisking continuously, then remove from the heat and stir in the peanut butter.
4. Place the chocolate in a bowl and pour over about a third of the hot peanut-butter filling. Mix well until the chocolate has melted and the filling is smooth and even. Pour the chocolate filling into the chilled cookie base, then cover the pie with cling film to stop a skin from forming on the filling, and place back in the fridge for 30–40 minutes to allow the filling to set. Cover the remaining peanut filling with cling film and set aside to cool.
5. In another bowl, whip the cream, either by hand or using a hand-held electric whisk, until it is thick and forms soft peaks. Once the remaining peanut-butter filling has completely cooled, fold in the whipped cream, ensuring it is mixed in well. Remove the pie from the fridge and top with this second part of the filling, then place back in the fridge to set for 40–50 minutes.
6. Next make the topping. Whip the cream and the icing sugar until the cream forms soft peaks, then spoon on top of the set pie filling and sprinkle with the chopped peanuts to finish.

HAZELNUT PRALINE MUFFINS

We never cool our muffins completely, but love to eat them when they're still a little bit warm. They're always devoured in minutes!

Makes 10–12 muffins

300g (10½oz) plain flour
145g (5oz) caster sugar
1 tbsp baking powder
½ tsp bicarbonate of soda
¼ tsp salt
250ml (9fl oz) whole milk
1 tsp vanilla essence
2 large eggs
85g (3oz) unsalted butter, melted
150g (5½oz) chocolate hazelnut spread
30g (1oz) hazelnuts, finely chopped

One 12-hole deep muffin tin

1. Preheat the oven to 170°C (325°F), Gas mark 3, and line the tin with muffin cases.
2. In a large bowl or the bowl of a freestanding electric mixer, sift together the flour, 115g (4oz) of the caster sugar, the baking powder, bicarbonate of soda and salt. Pour the milk and vanilla essence into a jug, break in the eggs and whisk together by hand.
3. Make a well in the centre of the dry ingredients and pour in the milk and eggs while mixing on a low speed, using either the freestanding mixer with the paddle attachment or a hand-held electric whisk. Scrape down the sides of the bowl occasionally and, on a medium-to-high speed, mix the batter until smooth. Add the melted butter and whisk a little more.
4. Add 80g (3oz) of the hazelnut spread to the muffin batter and mix thoroughly. Next spoon the batter into the prepared muffin cases, filling them about a quarter full. Spoon about 1 teaspoon of the remaining hazelnut spread into the middle of each muffin, then add the remaining batter, so that each case is about two-thirds full.
5. Sprinkle over the chopped hazelnuts and the remaining caster sugar. (It may seem like a generous amount of sugar, but it will create a lovely crust on the muffins once they are cooked.) Place in the oven and bake for 25–30 minutes or until the muffins are well risen and bounce back when lightly pressed. Allow to cool slightly in the tin before transferring to a wire rack.

COLA CUPCAKES

When we sold the soda range in our shops, Fridays meant Cola Cupcakes. They were really popular and loved by kids of all ages. We decorate them with cola bottles, which can be bought in most sweet shops and supermarket pick 'n' mix sections. Or you could use cola-flavoured jelly beans.

Makes 12–16 cupcakes

FOR THE SPONGE
80g (3oz) unsalted butter, softened
280g (10oz) caster sugar
240g (8½oz) plain flour
1 tbsp baking powder
¼ tsp salt
1 tbsp cola syrup
240ml (8½fl oz) milk
2 large eggs

FOR THE FROSTING
500g (1lb 2oz) icing sugar
160g (5½oz) unsalted butter, softened
2 tbsp cola syrup
50ml (1¾fl oz) whole milk
24–36 cola bottle sweets, to decorate (optional)

One or two 12-hole deep muffin tins

1. Preheat the oven to 190°C (375°F), Gas mark 5, and fill a muffin tin with muffin cases.
2. Using a hand-held electric whisk or a freestanding electric mixer with the paddle attachment, beat together the butter, sugar, flour, baking powder and salt on a low speed until the ingredients are well incorporated and have the texture of fine breadcrumbs.
3. Put the cola syrup and milk in a jug, break in the eggs and whisk by hand to combine. Pour three-quarters of the milk mixture into the dry ingredients and mix together on a low speed. Adjust the speed to medium and continue to mix until smooth and thick. Scrape down the sides of the bowl, add the remaining milk mixture and keep beating until everything is mixed in and the batter is smooth.
4. Divide the batter between the paper cases, filling them by about two-thirds. Any remaining batter can be used to fill up to four more cases in a second tin. Place in the oven and bake for 18– 20 minutes or until risen and springy to the touch. Leave to cool slightly before removing from the tin and placing on a wire rack to cool completely before frosting.
5. Using the electric whisk or freestanding mixer with the paddle attachment, beat the icing sugar with the butter on a low speed until no large lumps of butter are left and the mixture is still powdery. Stir together the cola syrup with the milk in a jug, then pour this into the butter and icing sugar mixture while beating slowly. Once added, increase the speed to high and whisk until soft and fluffy.
6. Spread a generous spoonful of frosting on to each cooled cupcake, then gently smooth over with a palette knife, making a swirl at the top and adding a couple of cola bottle sweets, if you wish.

CHOCOLATE CHIP WHOOPIE PIES

We love chocolate chip cookies, so decided to make them into a whoopie pie. You can use milk chocolate or dark chocolate chips, depending on your preference.

Makes 8–10 pies

FOR THE SPONGE

1 large egg
150g (5½oz) caster sugar
125g (4½oz) plain yoghurt
25ml (1fl oz) milk
¼ tsp vanilla essence
75g (2½oz) unsalted butter, melted
275g (10oz) plain flour
¾ tsp bicarbonate of soda
¼ tsp baking powder
150g (5½oz) dark chocolate chips (minimum 70% cocoa solids)

FOR THE FILLING

170g (6oz) unsalted butter, softened
2 tbsp cocoa powder
280g (10oz) icing sugar
220g (8oz) vanilla Marshmallow Fluff

1. Using a hand-held electric whisk or a freestanding electric mixer with the paddle attachment, whisk the egg and the sugar until pale and fluffy. Pour the yoghurt, milk and vanilla essence into a jug. Mix together by hand, then gradually add this to the egg mixture, whisking on a low speed until combined. Pour in the melted butter and mix again.

2. Sift together the flour, bicarbonate of soda and the baking powder, then add these dry ingredients to the batter in two stages, mixing thoroughly to ensure everything is well combined. Stir in the chocolate chips by hand, then place the finished batter in the fridge to allow to cool and set for 15–20 minutes.

3. In the meantime, preheat the oven to 170°C (325°F), Gas mark 3, and line two baking trays with baking parchment.

4. Spoon the batter on to the trays, making 16–20 mounds, each 3–5cm (1¼–2in) in diameter and 2–3cm (¾–1¼in) apart. Bake in the oven for 10–13 minutes or until a light-golden colour on top and the sponges bounce back when gently pressed. Allow to cool completely on a wire rack before you add the filling.

5. While the sponges are cooking, and using the electric whisk or freestanding mixer with the paddle attachment, mix together the butter, cocoa powder and the icing sugar on a low speed until smooth. Add the marshmallow fluff and continue to beat, on a high speed, until the frosting is soft and fluffy. Chill in the fridge for 30 minutes to firm up.

6. To assemble the whoopie pies, take one sponge and spread about 2 tablespoons of the filling on the flat side and then sandwich together with another sponge, with the flat side facing down. Continue doing this until all the sponge and frosting has been used.

CHEWY MONKEY BARS

Perfect for lunchboxes and as portable snacks, these bars are easy to make and require no baking. You can vary the nuts and dried fruits, but stick to the same weights and proportions that we've indicated in the recipe.

Makes 12 bars

120g (4oz) runny honey
60g (2oz) unsalted butter
60g (2oz) crunchy peanut
   butter
160g (5½oz) white mini
   marshmallows
1 tsp vanilla essence
100g (3½oz) rolled oats
175g (6oz) puffed rice cereal
175g (6oz) desiccated coconut
40g (1½oz) roasted unsalted
   peanuts, roughly chopped
40g (1½oz) glacé cherries,
   roughly chopped
100g (3½oz) dark chocolate chips
   (minimum 70% cocoa solids)
50g (1¾oz) chopped mixed nuts

One 22 x 31cm (9 x 12½in)
baking tray

1. Line the tray with baking parchment. Place the honey in a saucepan with the butter, peanut butter, marshmallows and vanilla essence and melt together over a low heat.
2. In a bowl, mix together the oats, rice cereal, coconut, peanuts, cherries and 70g (2½oz) of the chocolate chips. Pour the warm, melted ingredients over this dry mixture, stirring together thoroughly to make sure all of the dry ingredients are evenly coated. Press the mixture into the prepared baking tray.
3. Melt the remaining chocolate chips in a microwave or in a glass bowl over a pan of simmering water. Drizzle the melted chocolate over the top of the monkey bar mixture and sprinkle with the chopped mixed nuts, then leave in the fridge for about 1 hour to set. Once the mixture has set, it can be turned out on to a chopping board and sliced into 12 bars.

MAPLE AND PECAN LAYER CAKE

Maple syrup is a great sweetener, making the sponge in this cake really moist and the frosting lovely and rich.

Serves 10–12

FOR THE SPONGE
120g (4oz) unsalted butter, softened
400g (14oz) caster sugar
360g (12½oz) plain flour
1½ tbsp baking powder
¼ tsp salt
360ml (12½fl oz) whole milk
40ml (1½fl oz) maple syrup
3 large eggs
100g (3½oz) pecans, chopped

FOR THE FROSTING
240g (8½oz) unsalted butter
750g (1lb 10oz) icing sugar
60ml (2fl oz) whole milk
1 tbsp maple syrup
Pecan halves, to decorate

Three 20cm (8in) diameter loose-bottomed sandwich tins

1. Preheat the oven to 170°C (325°F), Gas mark 3, and line the base of the sandwich tins with baking parchment.
2. Using a hand-held electric whisk or a freestanding electric mixer with the paddle attachment, set on a low speed, mix together the butter, sugar, flour, baking powder and salt until the mixture reaches a crumb-like consistency.
3. In a jug mix together the milk, maple syrup and eggs by hand. With the whisk or mixer still on a low speed, pour the milk mixture into the dry ingredients and beat until everything is combined. Stir in the chopped pecans by hand.
4. Divide the cake batter equally between the three prepared cake tins, then place in the oven and bake for 20–25 minutes or until the sponges are a golden brown colour and bounce back when lightly pressed. Leave in the tins for a few minutes, then turn out and allow to cool completely on a wire rack before you add the frosting.
5. Using the electric whisk or freestanding mixer with the paddle attachment, slowly mix the butter and icing sugar until fully combined and sandy in texture. In a jug mix together the milk and maple syrup, then pour this into the butter and icing sugar, while mixing on a low speed. When all the liquid has been incorporated, adjust the speed to high and beat the frosting until soft and fluffy.
6. Once the sponge layers feel cold to the touch, you can assemble the cake. Place the first layer on a plate or cake card and top with 3–4 tablespoons of the frosting. Smooth the frosting out using a palette knife, adding a little more if needed.
7. Sandwich the second layer on top, then add more frosting, followed by the third layer of cake. Next frost the sides and top of the cake, covering it completely so that the no sponge is showing. Finally, decorate the top of the cake with pecan halves.

STRAWBERRY DAIQUIRI MINI CUPCAKES

An adult treat that we always serve at our shop-opening events and other special occasions.

Makes 24–30 mini cupcakes

FOR THE SPONGE
100ml (3½fl oz) white rum
170g (6oz) caster sugar
150g (5½oz) strawberries
40g (1½oz) unsalted butter, softened
120g (4oz) plain flour
1½ tsp baking powder
¼ tsp salt
1 large egg
120ml (4fl oz) whole milk
½ tsp vanilla essence

FOR THE FROSTING
80g (3oz) unsalted butter, softened
250g (9oz) icing sugar
½ tsp finely grated lime zest
4 tsp whole milk
Sliced strawberries, sprinkles or edible glitter, to decorate

One or two 24-hole mini muffin tins

1. Preheat the oven to 170°C (325°F), Gas mark 3, and fill a muffin tin with mini muffin cases.
2. Add the rum and 30g (1oz) of the sugar to a small saucepan and bring to the boil, allowing it to reduce by about half, then set aside to cool slightly. Hull and chop the strawberries into small pieces, then soak in the rum and sugar reduction for 30–40 minutes.
3. Meanwhile, using a freestanding electric mixer with the paddle attachment or a hand-held electric whisk, slowly mix together the butter, flour, remaining sugar, baking powder and salt. Mix until the ingredients have come together and resemble fine breadcrumbs.
4. In a jug whisk the egg, milk and vanilla essence together. With the mixer or electric whisk still running on a low speed, gradually pour the liquid mixture into the flour and butter and mix thoroughly, scraping down the sides of the bowl every now and then.
5. Drain the strawberries from the rum reduction, reserving the liquid, and place a few small pieces of strawberry in each cupcake case. Spoon the cake batter on top, filling each case by two-thirds. Any remaining batter can be spooned into one to six more paper cases in a second mini muffin tin.
6. Bake for 12–15 minutes or until the cupcakes are a light golden-brown colour and bounce back when lightly pressed. While they are still warm, spoon about ½ teaspoon of the rum reduction over each cake, then leave to cool completely before frosting.
7. Using the freestanding mixer or electric whisk, set on a low speed, beat together the butter, icing sugar and lime zest until combined and crumb-like in texture, then mix together the milk and 4 teaspoons of the reserved rum reduction in a jug. Pour the milk and rum into the butter and icing sugar mixture, still mixing on a low speed. When all the liquid has been incorporated, increase the speed to high and beat the frosting until soft and fluffy.
8. Smooth the frosting on to the cupcakes using a palette knife. These cupcakes can be topped with fresh chopped strawberries or, for a celebratory touch, a scattering of sprinkles or edible glitter.

PINA COLADA MINI CUPCAKES

Inspired by the classic tropical cocktail, serve these at parties and your guests will love them.

Makes 24–30 mini cupcakes

FOR THE SPONGE

100ml (3½fl oz) white rum
170g (6oz) caster sugar
4 slices of tinned pineapple
40g (1½oz) unsalted butter, softened
120g (4oz) plain flour
1½ tsp baking powder
¼ tsp salt
1 large egg
120ml (4fl oz) coconut milk
½ tsp vanilla essence

FOR THE FROSTING

80g (3oz) unsalted butter, softened
250g (9oz) icing sugar
4 tsp coconut milk
4 tsp white rum
5 tbsp desiccated coconut, to decorate

One or two 24-hole mini muffin tins

1. Preheat the oven to 170°C (325°F), Gas mark 3, and line a muffin tin with mini muffin cases.

2. Pour the rum into a small saucepan and add 30g (1oz) of the caster sugar. Bring to the boil and allow the liquid to reduce by about half, then set aside to cool slightly. Meanwhile, cut the pineapple rings into small pieces – about 8 pieces per slice, or 32 pieces in total – and soak the pineapple in the rum reduction for 30–40 minutes.

3. Using a hand-held electric whisk or a freestanding electric mixer with the paddle attachment, mix together the butter, remaining sugar, flour, baking powder and salt on a low speed until everything has come together and the mixture has a crumb-like consistency. Mix together the remaining ingredients for the sponge in a jug by hand, then with the mixer or whisk still on a low speed, gradually pour the liquid mixture into the flour and butter and beat together thoroughly, scraping down the sides of the bowl from time to time.

4. Drain the pineapple from the rum reduction, retaining the rum for later. Place a small piece of pineapple in each paper case, then spoon the cake batter on top, filling each up to two-thirds full. If you have any batter left over, place it in one to six cases in a second mini muffin tin.

5. Bake for 12–15 minutes or until the cupcakes are a light golden brown on top and bounce back when lightly pressed. While the cupcakes are still warm, spoon about ½ teaspoon of the rum reduction over each cake, then allow the cupcakes to cool completely while you make the frosting.

6. Mix the butter and icing sugar on a low speed, using either the electric whisk or freestanding mixer with the paddle attachment, until sandy in texture and no large lumps of butter remain. Whisk the coconut milk and rum together in a jug, then pour this into the butter and icing sugar while still mixing on a low speed. When all the liquid has been incorporated, increase the speed to high and beat the frosting until light and fluffy.

7. Spread the frosting on to the cupcakes using a palette knife, then dip the frosted cakes into the desiccated coconut, coating the tops completely.

BRANDY CHOCOLATE
MINI CUPCAKES

An indulgent cocktail cupcake that is perfect for parties or to accompany coffee at the end of a special meal.

Makes 24–30 mini cupcakes

FOR THE SPONGE
40g (1½oz) unsalted butter, softened
140g (5oz) caster sugar
100g (3½oz) plain flour
20g (¾oz) cocoa powder
1½ tsp baking powder
½ tsp finely grated orange zest
¼ tsp salt
1 large egg
50ml (1¾fl oz) brandy
80ml (3fl oz) whole milk

FOR THE FROSTING
75g (2½oz) unsalted butter, softened
225g (8oz) icing sugar
30g (1oz) cocoa powder
¾ tsp finely grated orange zest
15ml (½fl oz) whole milk
15ml (½fl oz) brandy
Sprinkles, chocolate shavings or edible glitter, to decorate (optional)

One or two 24-hole mini muffin tins

1. Preheat the oven to 170°C (325°F), Gas mark 3, and line a muffin tin with mini muffin cases.
2. Using a hand-held electric whisk or a freestanding electric mixer with the paddle attachment, slowly mix together the butter, sugar, flour, cocoa powder, baking powder, orange zest and salt. Keep mixing until the ingredients have come together and resemble fine breadcrumbs.
3. Break the egg into a jug, add the brandy and milk and mix together. With the mixer or whisk on a low speed, slowly pour the liquids into the dry ingredients and mix until smooth, scraping down the sides of the bowl to include every bit of the mixture.
4. Divide the cake batter between the muffin cases, filling each one two-thirds full. If any batter is left over, use it to fill up to six more paper cases in a second tin. Bake for 12–15 minutes or until the tops of the cupcakes bounce back when lightly pressed, then leave to cool completely on a wire rack before topping with the frosting.
5. Using the freestanding mixer or electric whisk, set on a low speed, mix together the butter, icing sugar, cocoa powder and orange zest until combined and sandy in consistency. Pour the milk and brandy into a jug, then pour this into the butter and icing sugar mixture, while still mixing on a low speed. When all the liquid is incorporated, increase the speed to high and beat the frosting until soft and fluffy.
6. Smooth the frosting on to the cupcakes using a palette knife and sprinkle with chocolate shavings, sprinkles or glitter (if using) for a pretty finish.

MOJITO MINI CUPCAKES

A fresh-tasting and zesty treat, these little cupcakes look pretty decorated with chopped fresh mint or lime zest.

Makes 24–30 mini cupcakes

FOR THE SPONGE

100ml (3½fl oz) white rum
170g (6oz) caster sugar
40g (1½oz) unsalted butter, softened
120g (4oz) plain flour
¼ tsp salt
1½ tsp baking powder
1 tsp finely grated lime zest
1 tsp finely grated lemon zest
1 tbsp finely chopped mint
1 large egg
120ml (4fl oz) whole milk
½ tsp vanilla essence

FOR THE FROSTING

80g (3oz) unsalted butter, softened
250g (9oz) icing sugar
¼ tsp finely grated lemon zest
¼ tsp finely grated lime zest
4 tsp whole milk
4 tsp white rum
1 tbsp caster sugar
1 tsp grated lime zest or finely chopped mint, to decorate

One or two 24-hole mini muffin tins

1. Preheat the oven to 170°C (325°F), Gas mark 3, and line a muffin tin with mini muffin cases.

2. In a small saucepan, bring the white rum and 30g (1oz) of the sugar to the boil, allowing it to reduce by about half, then set aside.

3. Using a hand-held electric whisk or a freestanding electric mixer with the paddle attachment, set on a low speed, beat together the butter, flour, salt, baking powder, lime and lemon zest, mint and remaining sugar. Mix until the ingredients have come together and are crumb-like in consistency.

4. Mix together the remaining ingredients for the sponge in a jug. With the mixer or whisk still on a low speed, gradually pour the liquid ingredients into the flour and butter mixture and mix thoroughly, scraping down the sides of the bowl.

5. Spoon the cake batter into the paper cases, filling each up to two-thirds full. Any remaining batter can be used to fill one to six more cases in a separate tin. Place in the oven and bake for 12–15 minutes or until the cupcakes are a light golden brown on top and springy to the touch.

6. While the cupcakes are still warm, spoon about ½ teaspoon of the rum reduction over each cake, then leave the cakes to cool completely on a wire rack before frosting.

7. Using the electric whisk or freestanding mixer with the paddle attachment, mix together the butter, icing sugar, lemon and lime zest on a low speed until combined and sandy in consistency. In a jug stir together the milk and rum, then pour this into the butter and icing sugar while still mixing on a low speed. When all the liquid ingredients have been incorporated, increase the speed to high and beat the frosting until light and fluffy.

8. Divide the frosting between the cupcakes, smoothing it on with a palette knife. To finish, mix the caster sugar with the grated lime zest or chopped mint in a small bowl, then sprinkle this on top of the frosted cupcakes.

SPICED APPLE CAKE WITH BROWN SUGAR FROSTING

A dark and rich cake that requires a little more time in the kitchen but looks and tastes wonderful. The flavoursome layers of apple sponge and brown-sugar meringue frosting are a delicious combination that will delight any birthday boy or girl.

Serves 14–16

FOR THE SPONGE
280g (10oz) unsalted butter, softened
2 Granny Smith apples
120ml (4fl oz) apple juice
500g (1lb 2oz) soft light brown sugar
2 tsp ground cinnamon
½ tsp freshly grated nutmeg
½ tsp ground ginger
4 large eggs
460g (1lb) plain flour
2½ tsp baking powder
2½ tsp bicarbonate of soda
½ tsp salt
120ml (4fl oz) soured cream
2 tsp vanilla essence
300g (10½oz) pecans, chopped

FOR THE FROSTING
6 large egg whites
250g (9oz) soft dark brown sugar
440g (15½oz) unsalted butter, chilled and cut into small cubes
Gold dragées, to decorate

Four 20cm (8in) diameter loose-bottomed sandwich tins

1. Preheat the oven to 170°C (325°F), Gas mark 3, and line the bases of the sandwich tins with baking parchment.
2. Melt 40g (1½oz) of the butter in a saucepan set over a low heat, then peel and core the apples and finely grate them. Weigh the grated apples (you need about 100g/3½oz) and add to the pan, along with the apple juice, 150g (5½oz) of the sugar and the ground spices, then cook until the apples are soft and the liquid has reduced by about three-quarters.
3. Using a hand-held electric whisk or a freestanding electric mixer with the paddle attachment, cream the remaining butter and sugar until pale and fluffy. Add one egg at a time, scraping down the bowl after each addition.
4. Sift together the flour, baking powder, bicarbonate of soda and salt, then add half of the dry ingredients with the soured cream and the vanilla essence to the creamed mixture. Mix well on a low speed, then mix in the remaining dry ingredients, increase the speed to high and beat until smooth.
5. Stir in the cooked apples and pecans by hand, making sure the apples are evenly distributed. Divide the mixture between the four tins and bake for approximately 20 minutes or until the sponge bounces back when lightly pressed. Allow to cool in the tins for a few minutes, then turn out on to a wire rack to cool fully before frosting.
6. While the sponges are cooking, place the egg whites and sugar in a glass bowl over a saucepan of simmering water. Using the hand-held electric whisk, beat on a high speed for 6–8 minutes or until the sugar has dissolved and the meringue has increased in volume and forms soft peaks.
7. Remove from the heat and whisk in the butter, adding 3–4 cubes at a time. Once all the butter has been added, whisk for a further 4–5 minutes or until the frosting is smooth and glossy. Set the frosting aside to cool for 45 minutes to 1 hour.
8. To assemble the cake, place the first layer of sponge on a plate or cake card and top with 3–4 tablespoons of frosting, smoothing it to the edges using a palette knife and adding a little more frosting if needed. Continue this process with the remaining three layers, leaving enough frosting to cover the sides and top of the cake and making sure no sponge is visible. Decorate with gold dragées, as shown in the photograph.

RAINY DAY TREATS

APPLE AND OATMEAL COOKIES

We usually bake these cookies until they're a light golden brown but if you prefer softer cookies, remove them from the oven as soon as they start to become golden. Perfect with a cup of tea or coffee, these keep in a sealed jar for several days.

Makes 10–12 cookies

135g (5oz) unsalted butter, softened
80g (3oz) caster sugar
80g (3oz) soft light brown sugar
1 large egg
½ tsp vanilla essence
190g (7oz) plain flour
½ tsp salt
¼ tsp ground cinnamon
½ tsp bicarbonate of soda
2 Granny Smith apples
60g (2oz) rolled oats

1. Preheat the oven to 170°C (325°F), Gas mark 3, and line two baking sheets with baking parchment.
2. Using a hand-held electric whisk or a freestanding electric mixer with the paddle attachment, cream together the butter and both types of sugar. Add the egg and vanilla essence and mix thoroughly on a medium speed. Sift together the flour, salt, cinnamon and bicarbonate of soda, then add these dry ingredients to the creamed mixture in two batches and mix thoroughly, in the mixer or by hand, until a dough forms.
3. Peel and finely grate the apples and squeeze all of the liquid out of them, discarding the liquid. Add the oats and 60g (2oz) of the grated apple to the cookie dough and stir in by hand.
4. Break off pieces of the dough (about 2 tablespoons in size), roll into balls and place on the prepared baking sheets. Allow five to six cookies per sheet, making sure to space them apart by 7–8cm (about 3in) as they will spread during cooking.
5. Place in the oven and bake for 15–20 minutes or until the cookies are a light golden brown. Leave on the sheets for about 10 minutes to cool and set, and then remove to a wire rack.

BANOFFEE CUPCAKES

Dulce de leche custard atop moist banana sponge, we decorate these cupcakes with shaved dark chocolate for added indulgence.

Makes 12–16 cupcakes

FOR THE SPONGE
80g (3oz) unsalted butter,
    softened
280g (10oz) caster sugar
240g (8½oz) plain flour
1 tbsp baking powder
¼ tsp salt
240ml (8½fl oz) whole milk
1 tsp vanilla essence
2 large eggs
2 ripe bananas

FOR THE TOPPING
500ml (18fl oz) whole milk
½ tsp vanilla essence
5 egg yolks
100g (3½oz) caster sugar
30g (1oz) plain flour
30g (1oz) cornflour
100g (3½oz) tinned caramel
    or *dulce de leche*
200ml (7fl oz) double cream
Shaved or grated chocolate,
    to decorate

*One or two 12-hole
    deep muffin tins
Piping bag (optional)*

1. Preheat the oven to 190°C (375°F), Gas mark 5, then fill a muffin tin with muffin cases and line a baking tray with cling film.

2. Using a hand-held electric whisk or a freestanding electric mixer with the paddle attachment, beat together the butter, sugar, flour, baking powder and salt on a low speed until the ingredients are well incorporated and have the texture of fine breadcrumbs.

3. In a jug, whisk together the milk, vanilla essence and eggs by hand. Pour three-quarters of this into the dry ingredients and mix well on a low speed, scraping the sides of the bowl to ensure the ingredients are all incorporated. Increase the speed to medium, add the rest of the milk mixture and beat until the batter is smooth, then peel and mash the bananas and stir in.

4. Divide the batter between the paper cases, filling each one by about two-thirds. Any remaining batter can be used to fill up to four more cases in a second tin. Bake the cupcakes in the oven for 18–20 minutes or until the sponge bounces back when lightly pressed. Leave to cool slightly before removing from the tin and placing on a wire rack to cool completely.

5. While the cupcakes are cooking, start making the custard cream topping. Place the milk in a saucepan with the vanilla essence and bring to the boil. In a separate bowl, mix together the egg yolks, sugar, flour and cornflour to make a paste, adding 1 tablespoon of the hot milk to loosen the mixture if it seems too thick.

6. When the milk has boiled, add 4–5 tablespoons to the paste and stir together, then pour this back into the pan with the remaining milk and return to the heat. Bring the mixture back up to the boil, whisking constantly, and continue to cook for a further minute to ensure the flour is cooked. Take the pan off the heat and stir in the caramel.

7. Pour the caramel custard into the prepared baking tray, cover the top with cling film and set aside to cool for 30–40 minutes. Once cooled, tip the custard into a large mixing bowl and beat with a wooden spoon to break up any lumps. In a separate bowl, whip the double cream to soft peaks, then fold the whipped cream into the caramel custard.

8. When the cupcakes are cold to the touch, pipe the caramel cream on top of each cake, or use a spoon to do this, if you prefer. Decorate with shaved or grated chocolate.

COFFEE AND CHOCOLATE LOAF

Dark, moist and delightfully rich. We like this plain, but you could add chocolate chips or chocolate coffee beans for a variation.

Serves 8–10

190g (7oz) unsalted butter,
  softened, plus extra
  for greasing
130g (4½oz) plain flour,
  plus extra for dusting
190g (7oz) soft light
  brown sugar
3 large eggs
60g (2oz) cocoa powder
1 tsp baking powder
20ml (¾fl oz) whole milk
1 tbsp strong coffee
  (brewed and cooled)

*One 8.5 x 17.5cm (3½ x 7in)
loaf tin with 7.5cm (3in) sides*

1. Preheat the oven to 170°C (325°F), Gas mark 3, then grease the loaf tin with butter and dust with flour.
2. Using a hand-held electric whisk or a freestanding electric mixer with the paddle attachment, cream the butter and sugar together until pale and fluffy. Add the eggs one at a time, mixing well after each addition and scraping down the sides of the bowl to make sure all the ingredients are mixed in properly.
3. Sift together the flour, cocoa powder and baking powder, then pour the milk into a jug, add the coffee and mix together. Add the dry ingredients to the cake batter in two batches, alternating with the coffee-flavoured milk. Mix well on a low speed after each addition and scrape down the sides of the bowl.
4. Once all the ingredients have been incorporated, increase the speed to medium-to-high to get a smooth and even batter, then pour the mixture into the prepared loaf tin.
5. Place in the oven and bake for approximately 1 hour or until the sponge is firm and a skewer inserted into the middle of the loaf comes out clean, with no cake batter sticking to it. Allow to cool for a while in the loaf tin before turning it out on to a cooling rack to cool completely.

WALNUT AND HONEY LOAF

This loaf has a wonderful honey syrup that soaks into the sponge and makes it incredibly moist and moreish. Walnuts and honey marry well, although pecans can be used instead of the walnuts if you like.

Serves 8–10

190g (7oz) unsalted butter,
    plus extra for greasing
190g (7oz) plain flour,
    plus extra for dusting
190g (7oz) caster sugar
3 eggs
1 tsp baking powder
¼ tsp salt
25g (1oz) plain yoghurt
1 tsp vanilla essence
2 tbsp runny honey
60g (2oz) walnuts,
    roughly chopped

*One 8.5 x 17.5cm (3½ x 7in)
loaf tin with 7.5cm (3in) sides*

1. Preheat the oven to 170°C (325°F), Gas mark 3, then grease the loaf tin with butter and dust with flour.
2. Using a hand-held electric whisk or a freestanding electric mixer with the paddle attachment, cream together the butter and sugar until pale and fluffy. Break in the eggs one at a time, whisking well before adding the next egg. Scrape down the sides of the bowl from time to time to make sure all the ingredients mix together properly.
3. Sift together the flour, baking powder and salt, then add these dry ingredients to the batter in two stages and mix on a low speed until just incorporated. Mix in the yoghurt, vanilla essence and half the honey, then stir in the walnuts by hand.
4. Pour or spoon the batter into the prepared loaf tin and bake for 50–60 minutes or until the sponge is firm and a skewer inserted into the centre of the cake comes out clean of any uncooked batter.
5. While the cake is cooking, place the remaining honey in a small saucepan with 50ml (1¾fl oz) of water and bring to the boil, allowing the syrup to reduce by about half. Pour the warm syrup over the cake when it comes out of the oven, then leave to cool in the tin before turning out on to a wire rack and allowing to cool completely before serving.

CHOCOLATE AND PEANUT BUTTER WHOOPIE PIES

Another whoopie pie offering, this time to satisfy chocolate and peanut butter lovers. We like crunchy peanut butter, but you may prefer to substitute smooth instead.

Makes 8–10 pies

FOR THE SPONGE

1 large egg
150g (5½oz) caster sugar
125g (4½oz) plain yoghurt
25ml (1fl oz) milk
¼ tsp vanilla essence
75g (2½oz) unsalted butter, melted
275g (10oz) plain flour
75g (2½oz) cocoa powder
¾ tsp bicarbonate of soda
¼ tsp baking powder
60g (2oz) crunchy peanut butter

FOR THE FILLING

170g (6oz) unsalted butter, softened
280g (10oz) icing sugar
220g (8oz) vanilla Marshmallow Fluff

1. Using a hand-held electric whisk or a freestanding electric mixer with the paddle attachment, cream together the egg and the sugar until pale and fluffy. Pour the yoghurt, milk and vanilla essence into a jug and stir together, then gradually add this to the egg mixture. Whisk on a low speed until combined, then pour in the melted butter and mix again.

2. Sift together the flour, cocoa powder, bicarbonate of soda and baking powder, then add half to the batter and mix well, on a low speed. Tip in the remaining half and beat together, then increase the speed to medium and mix until the batter is smooth. Add the peanut butter and mix in, then place the batter in the fridge and allow to cool and set for 20–30 minutes.

3. In the meantime, preheat the oven to 170°C (325°F), Gas mark 3, and line two baking trays with baking parchment.

4. Once the batter has cooled down, spoon the mix on to the prepared trays. Make 16–20 mounds, each 3–5cm (1¼–2in) in diameter and spaced 2–3cm (¾–1¼in) apart. Place the trays in the oven and bake for 10–13 minutes or until the sponges bounce back when gently pressed. Allow to cool completely on a wire rack before you add the filling.

5. While the sponges are baking, and using the electric whisk or freestanding mixer with the paddle attachment, slowly mix together the butter and the icing sugar until smooth. Add the marshmallow and once the fluff has been mixed in, increase the speed to high and beat until light and fluffy. Chill in the fridge for 30 minutes to firm up.

6. To finish, spread the flat side of one sponge with about 1 tablespoon of the peanut butter filling, then sandwich another sponge on top, with the flat side down. Continue sandwiching together the remaining sponges with the rest of the filling.

BLACK AND WHITE CHOCOLATE CHEESECAKE BARS

**These black-and-white bars taste as good as they look!
Rich cocoa and cheesecake is one of our favourite combinations.**

Makes 12–15 bars

FOR THE BASE
250g (9oz) unsalted butter
420g (15oz) caster sugar
2 eggs
380g (13oz) plain flour
60g (2oz) cocoa powder
1 tsp bicarbonate of soda
½ tsp salt

FOR THE TOPPING
80g (3oz) white chocolate chips
300g (10½oz) full-fat cream
  cheese (such as Philadelphia)
60g (2oz) icing sugar
1 large egg

*One 23 x 30cm (9 x 12in)
baking tray*

1. Using a hand-held electric whisk or a freestanding electric mixer with the paddle attachment, cream the butter and sugar together until light and fluffy. Add the eggs one at a time, mixing thoroughly after each addition and scraping down the sides of the bowl to make sure every bit of the mixture is incorporated.

2. Sift together the remaining ingredients, then tip these into the batter in two batches, mixing in the freestanding mixer or folding in by hand.

3. Cut off approximately one-quarter of the dough, cover with cling film and place in the fridge. Line the baking tray with baking parchment, then press the remaining dough into the tray and allow it to set in the fridge for 20–30 minutes.

4. Meanwhile, preheat the oven to 170°C (325°F), Gas mark 3.

5. Remove the base from the fridge and bake for 20–25 minutes. Allow to cool completely in the tin before adding the topping, but keep the oven on for cooking the finished cheesecake.

6. Melt the chocolate in a glass bowl over a saucepan of simmering water, then remove from the heat and allow to cool slightly. Using the electric whisk or freestanding mixer with the paddle attachment, mix the cream cheese and sugar until smooth. Add the egg and mix thoroughly, then stir the melted chocolate into the cheesecake mixture by hand.

7. Spread the mixture on to the cooled base, then remove the reserved dough from the fridge and crumble in large pieces over the cheesecake.

8. Bake for approximately 25 minutes or until the cheesecake has set, then allow to cool completely before placing in the fridge for a few hours to set. Once set, cut the cheesecake into squares or rectangles to serve.

APPLE CRUMBLE CUPCAKES

This recipe involves a few stages for the more experienced baker to enjoy. The result will not disappoint: tangy apple, custard and crumble all on top of Hummingbird's light sponge.

Makes 12–16 cupcakes

FOR THE SPONGE

80g (3oz) unsalted butter
softened
280g (10oz) caster sugar
240g (8½oz) plain flour
1 tbsp baking powder
¼ tsp salt
½ tsp ground cinnamon
2 large eggs
240ml (8½fl oz) whole milk
¼ tsp vanilla essence

FOR THE FILLING

5 green eating apples
(such as Golden Delicious)
30g (1oz) unsalted butter,
softened
50g (1¾oz) soft light brown sugar
¼ tsp ground cinnamon

FOR THE CUSTARD TOPPING

500ml (18fl oz) whole milk
½ tsp vanilla essence
5 large egg yolks
200g (7oz) caster sugar
30g (1oz) plain flour
30g (1oz) cornflour
200ml (7fl oz) double cream

1. Preheat the oven to 190°C (375°F), Gas mark 5, then fill a muffin tin with muffin cases, line a baking tray with baking parchment and a second tray with cling film.

2. First make the apple filling. Peel, core and chop the apples into 1cm (½in) pieces. Melt the butter in a saucepan over a low heat, then add the apples, sugar and cinnamon. Give this a good stir to make sure the apples are coated in the spice mixture, then stew gently until the apples are soft and cooked through, but not mushy. Set them aside to cool while you prepare the batter for the cupcakes.

3. Using a hand-held electric whisk or a freestanding electric mixer with the paddle attachment, beat together the butter, sugar, flour, baking powder, salt and cinnamon on a low speed until the ingredients are well incorporated and have the texture of fine breadcrumbs.

4. Break the eggs into a jug, pour in the milk and vanilla essence and whisk together. With the mixer or electric whisk running on a low speed, add three-quarters of the milk mixture to the dry ingredients and beat well together, scraping down the sides of the bowl to make sure all the ingredients are well incorporated. Add the rest of the milk mixture and beat again, on a medium speed, until the batter is smooth.

5. Spoon the batter into the muffin cases, filling each one up to two-thirds full. Using a teaspoon, put about 2 teaspoons of the apple mixture into the centre of each case. This will sink into the cupcake batter. If any of the batter and cooked apples are left over, use them to fill up to four more paper cases in a second muffin tin.

6. Place the cupcakes in the oven and bake for 18–20 minutes or until the sponges feel springy to the touch. Leave to cool slightly before removing from the tin and placing on a wire rack to cool completely while you make the custard and crumble toppings.

7. To make the custard topping, pour the milk and vanilla essence into a clean saucepan and bring to the boil. In a bowl, mix together the egg yolks, sugar, flour and cornflour to make a paste. Add 1 tablespoon of the hot milk to thin the paste if it seems too thick.

FOR THE CRUMBLE TOPPING

55g (2oz) plain flour
55g (2oz) rolled oats
Pinch of ground cinnamon
55g (2oz) unsalted butter,
   chilled and cut into
   small cubes
40g (1½oz) soft light
   brown sugar

*One or two 12-hole deep
muffin tins*

8. When the milk has boiled, mix 4–5 tablespoons with the paste, then add this to the remaining milk in the pan and return to the hob. Bring back up to the boil, whisking constantly as the mixture heats. Continue to cook for a further minute to ensure the flour is cooked, then remove the pan from the heat. Pour the custard on to the baking tray lined with cling film, cover with more cling film and set aside to cool for 30–40 minutes.

9. For the crumble topping, first mix the flour, oats and cinnamon in a bowl. Add the butter and rub in, using your fingertips, until all of the ingredients have come together in an even, crumb-like consistency. Finally, add the sugar, making sure it is evenly mixed in.

10. Spread the crumble mix on the paper-lined baking tray and bake in the oven for about 15 minutes, checking at regular intervals and gently stirring the crumbs around to make sure they brown evenly. Once the crumbs are golden, remove them from the oven and set aside to cool completely.

11. Tip the cooled custard into a large bowl and beat with a wooden spoon to break up any lumps. In a separate bowl whip the double cream, either by hand or using the electric whisk, until it forms soft peaks. Fold the whipped cream into the custard, making sure the mix is smooth and even. To finish, top the cupcakes with the custard cream and then sprinkle generously with the crumble mixture.

CHOCOLATE AND
CHESTNUT BISCUIT BARS

A sophisticated version of our famous Refrigerator Bars, we love the wintry taste of roast chestnuts with chocolate.

Makes 12 bars

200g (7oz) unsalted butter
100g (3½oz) golden syrup
50g (1¾oz) cocoa powder
350g (12oz) milk chocolate
  digestive biscuits
100g (3½oz) ready-cooked
  chestnuts, sliced
50g (1¾oz) dried cranberries
50g (1¾oz) mixed sultanas
  and raisins

*One 22 x 31cm (9 x 12½in)
baking tray*

1. Line the baking tray with baking parchment, then place the butter and golden syrup in a saucepan and melt together over a low heat. Once melted, stir in the cocoa powder until there are no lumps and the mixture is smooth.
2. Roughly break up the chocolate biscuits into a large bowl and add the chestnut slices and dried fruit. Pour the chocolate syrup over the biscuits, fruit and nuts, stirring together to make sure all the ingredients are coated in it.
3. Press the mixture into the prepared tin and place in the fridge to set for approximately 2 hours, or preferably overnight. Once the mixture has set, turn it out on to a chopping board and slice into bars.

HOT-CHOCOLATE CUPCAKES

Another appearance from our popular hot drinks range, we like to eat these whilst sipping from a cup of thick, piping-hot chocolate for double indulgence!

Makes 12–16 cupcakes

FOR THE SPONGE
240ml (8½fl oz) whole milk
25g (1oz) hot-chocolate powder
80g (3oz) unsalted butter, softened
280g (10oz) caster sugar
240g (8½oz) plain flour
1 tbsp baking powder
¼ tsp salt
2 large eggs

FOR THE FROSTING
60ml (2fl oz) whole milk
30g (1oz) hot-chocolate powder
500g (1lb 2oz) icing sugar
160g (5½oz) unsalted butter, softened

One or two 12-hole deep muffin tins

1. Preheat the oven to 190°C (375°F), Gas mark 5, and fill a muffin tin with muffin cases.
2. Gently warm the milk, without boiling it, and add the hot-chocolate powder, stirring until dissolved, then set aside and allow to cool.
3. Using a hand-held electric whisk or a freestanding electric mixer with the paddle attachment, slowly whisk together the butter, sugar, flour, baking powder and salt until they resemble fine breadcrumbs.
4. Pour the chocolate-flavoured milk into a jug and whisk in the eggs. Next pour three-quarters of this mixture into the dry ingredients and, still on a low speed, mix to combine. Increase the speed to medium and continue to mix until smooth and thick. Scrape down the sides of the bowl, then pour in the remaining milk mixture and continue mixing until all the ingredients are incorporated and the batter is smooth once again.
5. Fill each muffin case up to two-thirds full with the batter. If there is any left over, use it to fill up to four more cases in another muffin tin. Place in the oven and bake for 18–20 minutes or until risen and springy to the touch, then leave to cool completely while you make the frosting.
6. Slightly warm the milk to dissolve the hot-chocolate powder, making sure there are no crystals left in the milk, then leave to cool down completely.
7. Using the electric whisk or freestanding mixer with the paddle attachment, beat the icing sugar with the butter on a low speed until sandy in texture and no large lumps of butter remain. Still mixing on a low speed, gradually pour in the chocolate milk. Once this has been added, increase the speed to high and whisk until light and fluffy.
8. To finish, divide the frosting between the cold cupcakes, smoothing it on with a palette knife and giving a swirl to the tops.

BUTTERSCOTCH PECAN CHEESECAKE

Thick and creamy, chock-full of tasty pecans, and topped with a fabulous butterscotch glaze.

Serves 8–12

FOR THE BISCUIT BASE
220g (8oz) digestive biscuits
100g (3½oz) unsalted butter, melted

FOR THE CHEESECAKE TOPPING
700g (1½lb) full-fat cream cheese (such as Philadelphia)
120g (4oz) caster sugar
1 tsp vanilla essence
3 large eggs
80g (3oz) pecans, finely chopped plus 10–12 pecan halves, to decorate

FOR THE BUTTERSCOTCH GLAZE
60g (2oz) unsalted butter
45g (1½oz) soft light brown sugar
2 tbsp whole milk
120g (4oz) icing sugar
1 tsp vanilla essence

One 20cm (8in) diameter spring-form cake tin

1. Line the base of the cake tin with baking parchment, then, in a food processor, whiz the digestive biscuits into fine crumbs using the blade attachment. Or, if you prefer, pop the biscuits in a plastic bag and crush them with a rolling pin.

2. Place the biscuit crumbs in a bowl, add the melted butter and mix together with a spoon. Pour the buttery crumbs into the lined cake tin, pressing them into the base of the tin, then place in the fridge for 20–30 minutes to cool and set.

3. Meanwhile, preheat the oven to 160°C (320°F), Gas mark 3, and prepare the cheesecake topping.

4. Using a hand-held electric whisk or a freestanding electric mixer with the paddle attachment, mix together the cream cheese, sugar and vanilla essence on a medium speed until smooth. Add the eggs one at a time, mixing thoroughly after each addition and scraping down the sides of the bowl. Stir in the chopped pecan nuts by hand and then pour the cheesecake mix on to the chilled biscuit base.

5. Wrap the cake tin in foil (see the tip on page 80) and place in a roasting tin. Fill with water to about 5mm (¼in) from the top of the cake tin, creating a water bath for the cheesecake to bake in, to prevent it cracking on top while cooking. Place in the oven and bake for 35–45 minutes or until the cheesecake is a light golden colour, especially around the edges, firm to the touch and with only a slight wobble in the middle.

6. Allow the cheesecake to cool down at room temperature while still in the tin, and then place in the fridge to set for a few hours.

7. When the cheesecake is fully chilled, make the butterscotch glaze. Put the butter, sugar and milk in a small saucepan and bring it to the boil. Remove from the heat, stir in the icing sugar and vanilla essence, then whisk until the glaze is smooth.

8. Pour the glaze on top of the cheesecake and decorate the top with the pecan halves. Place in the fridge to set for a few hours, or overnight if possible. Remove from the cake tin before serving.

HALLOWEEN & BONFIRE NIGHT

RED VELVET CUPCAKES

After seven years, red velvets are still our bestselling flavour!
Remember to use the correct red food colouring for the sponge
and full-fat cream cheese for the frosting. The quantities can all
be doubled if you want to convert this recipe into a 20cm (8in)
three-layer cake.

Makes 12–16 cupcakes

FOR THE SPONGE

120g (4oz) unsalted butter,
  softened
300g (10½oz) caster sugar
2 large eggs
20g (¾oz) cocoa powder
40ml (1½fl oz) red food
  colouring (such as Dr Oetker)
1 tsp vanilla essence
300g (10½oz) plain flour
1 tsp salt
240ml (8½fl oz) buttermilk
1 tbsp white wine vinegar
1 tsp bicarbonate of soda

FOR THE FROSTING

100g (3½oz) unsalted butter,
  softened
600g (1lb 5oz) icing sugar
250g (9oz) full-fat cream
  cheese (such as Philadelphia)
Coloured sprinkles,
  to decorate (optional)

*One or two 12-hole deep
muffin tins*

1. Preheat the oven to 190°C (375°F), Gas mark 5, and line a muffin tin with muffin cases.

2. Using a hand-held electric whisk or a freestanding electric mixer with the paddle attachment, cream the butter and sugar together until pale and fluffy. Break in the eggs one at a time, beating thoroughly after each addition and mixing in the scrapings from the sides of the bowl.

3. In a separate, small bowl, stir together the cocoa powder, food colouring and vanilla essence to form a paste. Add the paste to the batter, mixing thoroughly until the paste is completely incorporated.

4. Sift together the flour and salt in another bowl, then add the flour to the batter in two batches, alternating with the buttermilk and mixing thoroughly after each addition. Lastly, in another bowl, mix the vinegar and bicarbonate of soda together by hand and add it to the cake batter, mixing it in until it is fully incorporated.

5. Spoon the batter into the paper cases, so that they are two-thirds full, using any remaining batter to fill up to four more cases in another tin. Place in the oven and bake for 18–20 minutes or until the sponge bounces back when lightly pressed. Allow the cupcakes to cool for a short while in the tin, then place on a wire rack to cool completely before you frost them.

6. Using the electric whisk or freestanding mixer with the paddle attachment, and mixing on a low speed, beat the butter and icing sugar together until no large lumps of butter remain and the mixture is sandy in texture. Add the cream cheese and mix together slowly until everything is incorporated, then increase the speed to medium and beat the frosting until it is soft and fluffy.

7. Cover all but one of the cupcakes with 2 tablespoons of the cream cheese frosting, smoothing it down with a palette knife and making a swirl in the middle of the frosting for a decorative finish.

8. Place the remaining cupcake in a food processor and blitz into fine crumbs, then sprinkle the frosted cupcakes with the red crumbs. Or you can use coloured sprinkles instead, if you prefer.

CHOCOLATE CHUNK PECAN PIE

This variation on pecan pie has become our new favourite. Chocolate and pecans are perfect for each other, especially when surrounded by the sweet gooey traditional pecan-pie filling.

Serves 8–10

FOR THE PASTRY
110g (4oz) unsalted butter, softened
225g (8oz) plain flour, plus extra for dusting
80g (3oz) caster sugar
1 large egg

FOR THE FILLING
110g (4oz) unsalted butter, softened
225g (8oz) soft light brown sugar
110g (4oz) golden syrup
3 large eggs
260g (9oz) pecans, roughly chopped, plus 16 pecan halves
85g (3oz) dark chocolate chips (minimum 70% cocoa solids)

One 23cm (9in) diameter loose-bottomed tart tin

1. Using a freestanding electric mixer with the paddle attachment, mix together the butter and flour on a low speed until crumb-like in consistency. Add the sugar and then the egg, mixing gently just to incorporate. Alternatively, place the butter and flour in a separate bowl and rub together using your fingertips, then stir in the sugar, followed by the egg.
2. When a dough starts to form, take it out of the bowl and knead gently on a floured work surface to bring it together. Wrap the pastry in cling film and place in the fridge to rest for 20–30 minutes.
3. Once the pastry has rested, roll it out on a lightly floured worktop so that it is about 5mm (¼in) thick and large enough to fit your tart tin.
4. Line the tart tin with the pastry, gently pressing it down into the base and sides of the tin. Using a sharp knife, cut away any excess pastry so that it is level with the edge of the tin, then prick the base of the pastry a few times with the point of the knife. Put the pastry case back in the fridge to rest for another 20–30 minutes.
5. In the meantime, preheat the oven to 150°C (300°F), Gas mark 2, and place a baking sheet in the oven to heat up.
6. Once the pastry case has rested, line it with baking parchment and fill with baking beans and then place in the oven to bake 'blind' for 10 minutes. Carefully remove the baking beans, along with the parchment, and bake the tart case for another 10 minutes. Remove from the oven and set aside to cool while you make the filling.
7. In a saucepan over a low heat, melt the butter, sugar and golden syrup together. Once melted, set aside to cool. Whisk together the eggs in a bowl, just to break them up, then pour the melted ingredients into the eggs, stirring continuously until everything is combined.
8. Scatter the chopped pecans and chocolate chips over the base of the tart case and pour the liquid filling on top, then decorate with the pecan halves.
9. Place the pie carefully on to the hot baking sheet (this will help the base of the pie to bake evenly). Place in the oven and bake for 30 minutes, then reduce the temperature to 140°C (275°F), Gas mark 1, and bake for another 20 minutes. When cooked, the pie filling should be set, with a

BUTTERSCOTCH MARSHMALLOW BARS

We love how the pink and white mini marshmallows melt together in these bars. They're unlikely to last long – your friends just won't be able to resist.

Makes 10–12 bars

FOR THE BASE
150g (5½oz) plain flour
40g (1½oz) icing sugar
120g (4oz) unsalted butter,
  softened

FOR THE TOPPING
100g (3½oz) pink and white
  mini marshmallows
210g (7½oz) caster sugar
150g (5½oz) soft light
  brown sugar
190g (7oz) golden syrup
70g (2½oz) unsalted butter
60ml (2fl oz) double cream
1 tsp vanilla essence
60g (2oz) crunchy peanut butter
30g (1oz) mixed chopped nuts

One 22 x 31cm (9 x 12½in)
baking tray

1. Preheat the oven to 170°C (325°F), Gas mark 3, and line the baking tray with baking parchment.
2. Using a freestanding electric mixer with the paddle attachment, mix together the flour, icing sugar and butter until a dough forms. Alternatively, rub the butter with the flour and icing sugar by hand.
3. Press the dough into the prepared baking tray, making a slight lip around the edge to keep the liquid filling from pouring over the sides of the tray. Bake the base for approximately 20 minutes, or until the edges are a light golden brown and the middle is pale but cooked, then remove from the oven and allow to cool slightly.
4. Place the marshmallows on top of the baked base, spreading them out evenly, then place both types of sugar in a saucepan, along with the golden syrup and 240ml (8½fl oz) of water, and bring to the boil.
5. Allow the mixture to boil until the sugar reaches the soft-ball stage (see the tip on page 108), then remove the pan from the heat and stir in the butter. Bring the butterscotch back up to the boil and allow to bubble away for approximately 3 minutes.
6. Take the pan off the heat and stir in the double cream, vanilla essence and peanut butter. Stir continuously until the peanut butter has melted into the butterscotch, then pour the mixture on to the base, making sure that the marshmallows are completely coated in the sauce.
7. Sprinkle the chopped nuts over the top and allow to set at room temperature for a few hours, or preferably overnight. Once set, slice into 10–12 bars and serve.

STICKY TOFFEE CUPCAKES

Rich, dark, date-filled sponge with a toffee frosting – these cupcakes are even more delicious than the traditional steamed pudding.

Makes 12–16 cupcakes

FOR THE SPONGE

180g (6½oz) pitted and
   chopped dates
180ml (6½fl oz) boiling water
80g (3oz) unsalted butter,
   softened
150g (5½oz) soft light
   brown sugar
2 large eggs
180g (6½oz) plain flour
½ tsp baking powder
1 tsp bicarbonate of soda
¼ tsp salt
1 tsp vanilla essence

FOR THE FROSTING

160g (5½oz) unsalted butter,
   softened
500g (1lb 2oz) icing sugar
50ml (1¾fl oz) whole milk
100g (3½oz) tinned caramel
   or *dulce de leche*
12–16 dates, pitted and chopped,
   or small pieces of soft toffee,
   to decorate (optional)

*One or two 12-hole
deep muffin tins*

1. Place the chopped dates in a bowl, pour over the boiling water and leave to soak for approximately 20 minutes.
2. Meanwhile, preheat the oven to 190°C (375°F), Gas mark 5, and line a muffin tin with muffin cases.
3. Using a hand-held electric whisk or a freestanding electric mixer with the paddle attachment, beat the butter and sugar together until soft and fluffy. Break the eggs in one at a time, scraping down the sides of the bowl and mixing well on a medium speed after adding each egg.
4. Sift together the flour, baking powder, bicarbonate of soda and salt. Add these dry ingredients in three batches to the egg and butter mix, then adjust the speed to medium-to-high and continue mixing until the batter is smooth and even.
5. Scrape around the sides and bottom of the bowl to pick up any ingredients that might not be mixed in, then beat again briefly to ensure everything is well incorporated. Next add the vanilla essence to the date mixture and mix this into the cake batter by hand, making sure the dates are evenly dispersed throughout the batter.
6. Fill each paper case up to two-thirds full with the batter. Any remaining batter can be used to fill one to four more cases in a second muffin tin. Bake in the oven for 18–20 minutes or until risen and springy to the touch. Leave to cool slightly before removing from the tin and placing on a wire rack to cool completely before frosting.
7. Using the electric whisk or freestanding mixer with the paddle attachment, mix together the butter and icing sugar on a low speed until sandy in texture and no large lumps of butter remain.
8. Still mixing on a low speed, gradually add the milk and mix in well, then increase the speed to medium-to-high and beat until light and fluffy. Finally, add the tinned caramel, beating it in thoroughly to ensure the frosting is evenly mixed.
9. Spoon generous amounts of the frosting on to each cupcake, then gently smooth over with a palette knife, making a swirl at the top, if you wish. To finish, scatter over the chopped dates or toffee pieces (if using).

SPIDERWEB CHEESECAKE

A perfect addition to spooky Halloween festivities that children will love, you could even add spider decorations to this cheesecake for a full spider-web effect.

Serves 8–12

FOR THE BISCUIT BASE
220g (8oz) digestive biscuits
100g (3½oz) unsalted butter,
    melted

FOR THE CHEESECAKE TOPPING
4 leaves of gelatine
600g (1lb 5oz) full-fat cream
    cheese (such as Philadelphia)
110g (4oz) caster sugar
1 tsp vanilla essence
½ tsp finely grated lemon zest
200ml (7fl oz) double cream
60g (2oz) dark chocolate
    (minimum 70% cocoa solids)

*One 20cm (8in) diameter
    spring-form cake tin
Piping bag with a fine (no. 2)
    writing nozzle*

1. Line the base of the cake tin with baking parchment, then, in a food processor, whiz the digestive biscuits into fine crumbs using the blade attachment. Alternatively, place the biscuits in a plastic bag, seal it shut and crush with a rolling pin.
2. Tip the biscuit crumbs into a bowl, pour over the melted butter and mix together with a spoon. Pour the buttery crumbs into the lined cake tin, pressing them into the base of the tin, then place in the fridge for 20–30 minutes to cool and set while you make the topping.
3. Place the gelatine leaves in a bowl of tepid water to soften. Using a hand-held electric whisk or a freestanding electric mixer with the paddle attachment, mix together the cream cheese, sugar, vanilla essence and lemon zest until smooth. In a separate bowl, whisk the double cream until it forms soft peaks.
4. In a small saucepan, on a very low heat, melt approximately 200g (7oz) of the cream cheese mixture. Allow it to warm slightly, then remove from the heat, add the softened gelatine and let it melt in the cream cheese.
5. Add the remaining, cold cream cheese to the warm mixture in the pan, mixing it in 3 tablespoons at a time and stirring continuously. Carefully fold the whipped cream into the cheesecake mixture and then pour on to the prepared base in the tin. Smooth down the top of the cheesecake using a palette knife.
6. Break the chocolate into a glass bowl and melt over a pan of simmering water, then remove from the heat and allow to cool. Pour the chocolate into the piping bag and pipe on to the cheesecake in evenly spaced concentric circles. Using a toothpick or the point of a sharp knife, draw a fine line from the centre circle to the outer circle to create the spiderweb effect. Clean the toothpick or skewer after drawing each line.
7. Place the finished cheesecake in the fridge and allow it to set for a couple of hours, or preferably overnight.

PUMPKIN WHOOPIE PIES

Pumpkin is a traditional Halloween flavour in America and is increasingly popular over here. These whoopie pies are a great alternative to pumpkin pie and the purée makes the sponge deliciously moist.

Makes 8–10 whoopie pies

FOR THE SPONGE
120ml (4fl oz) sunflower oil
200g (7oz) soft light brown sugar
½ tsp vanilla essence
1 large egg
100ml (3½fl oz) tinned
　pumpkin purée
250g (9oz) plain flour
½ tsp baking powder
½ tsp bicarbonate of soda
½ tsp salt
1 tsp ground cinnamon
1 tsp ground ginger

FOR THE FILLING
85g (3oz) unsalted butter,
　softened
150g (5½oz) icing sugar, plus
　extra for dusting
80g (3oz) full-fat cream cheese
　(such as Philadelphia)
100g (3½oz) vanilla
　Marshmallow Fluff

1. Preheat the oven to 170°C (325°F), Gas mark 3, and line two baking trays with baking parchment.
2. Using a hand-held electric whisk or a freestanding electric mixer with the paddle attachment, mix together the sunflower oil, sugar and vanilla essence until combined and light in colour. Tip in the egg and pumpkin purée and mix until all the ingredients are incorporated.
3. Sift together the remaining ingredients and add these to the liquid mixture in two batches, mixing together thoroughly on a medium speed until an even batter forms.
4. Spoon the batter on to the prepared trays in 16–20 mounds, each 3–5cm (1¼–2in) in diameter. Remember the whoopie pies will spread during cooking, so keep them 2–3cm (¾–1¼in) apart. Place in the oven and bake for 10–13 minutes or until they are a golden colour and the sponge bounces back when lightly touched. Allow to cool completely before filling.
5. Using the electric whisk or freestanding mixer with the paddle attachment, mix together the butter and the icing sugar on a low speed until smooth. Add the cream cheese and continue mixing on a low speed. Once the ingredients are combined, increase the speed to high and beat for approximately 1 minute. Add the marshmallow fluff and beat the filling until it is light and fluffy, then place in the fridge for 30–40 minutes to set slightly.
6. To assemble the whoopie pies, take one sponge and spread roughly 1 tablespoon of the filling on to the flat side, adding a little more if needed. Then stick another sponge on top (flat side down) to create a sandwich. Repeat with the remaining ingredients. Dust the whoopie pies with icing sugar to serve.

APPLE AND CURRANT CRUMBLE BARS

We love using currants for this recipe, but other small dried fruits can be used instead, just keep to the same weight as specified in the recipe.

Makes 12 bars

200g (7oz) plain flour
1 tsp baking powder
¼ tsp salt
200g (7oz) unsalted butter, softened
250g (9oz) soft light brown sugar
120g (4oz) rolled oats
300g (10½oz) Granny Smith apples
4 tbsp cornflour
3 tsp ground cinnamon
1 tsp ground nutmeg
1 tsp ground ginger
175g (6oz) currants

One 22 x 31cm (9 x 12½in) baking tray

1. Preheat the oven to 170°C (325°F), Gas mark 3, and line the tray with baking parchment.
2. Sift the flour, baking powder and salt into a large bowl, add the butter and rub together until the consistency of breadcrumbs, then stir in the sugar and the rolled oats. If you prefer, you can mix together the dry ingredients with the butter in a freestanding electric mixer with the paddle attachment, then stir in the sugar and oats by hand. After mixing, press half of the mixture into the prepared tray, and set aside.
3. Peel and core the apples, then cut into slices and mix together with the cornflour and ground spices. Place the spice-coated apple slices in lines on the top of the oat mixture in the base of the tray, then sprinkle over the currants. Spoon the remaining mix over the apples and currants and press down gently.
4. Place in the oven and bake for 30–40 minutes or until the mixture is golden brown. Allow to cool completely in the baking tray before cutting into slices to serve.

BEETROOT AND CHOCOLATE CUPCAKES

We first made these for the Portobello Road Market's annual English Roots Festival, and they soon became very popular. Chocolate and beetroot go really well together, do try it!

Makes 12–16 cupcakes

FOR THE SPONGE
200g (7oz) plain flour
50g (1¾oz) cocoa powder
1½ tsp baking powder
½ tsp ground cinnamon
½ tsp salt
250g (9oz) caster sugar
300g (10½oz) cooked and
   peeled beetroot
3 large eggs
200ml (7fl oz) sunflower oil
1 tsp vanilla essence

FOR THE FROSTING
600g (1lb 5oz) icing sugar
100g (3½oz) unsalted butter,
   softened
250g (9oz) full-fat cream cheese
   (such as Philadelphia)
Edible Halloween-themed shapes,
   to decorate (optional)

*One or two 12-hole
deep muffin tins*

1. Preheat the oven to 190°C (375°F), Gas mark 5, and line a muffin tin with muffin cases.
2. Sift together the flour, cocoa powder, baking powder, cinnamon and salt, then stir in the caster sugar. Using a food processor, with the blade attachment, purée the beetroot until liquid and smooth, then add the eggs one by one, blitzing between each addition.
3. With the motor running on the food processor, gradually pour in the oil and vanilla essence, mixing until fully combined.
4. Gradually pour the beetroot mixture into the bowl with the dry ingredients, mixing it in using a hand-held electric whisk and beating until all ingredients are combined and the batter is smooth.
5. Divide the batter between the muffin cases, filling each one up to two-thirds full. If any batter is left over, use it to fill one to four more paper cases in a separate tin. Place in the oven and bake for 18–20 minutes or until the sponges are risen and bounce back when you press them lightly. Leave in the tin for a few minutes, then remove to a wire rack to cool completely while you prepare the frosting.
6. Using the electric whisk or a freestanding electric mixer with the paddle attachment, whisk the icing sugar with the butter on a low speed until fully combined and still powdery in consistency. Add the cream cheese and mix on a medium-to-high speed until the frosting is light, fluffy and smooth.
7. Once the cupcakes have cooled down, divide the frosting between them, smoothing and swirling with a palette knife. If you want to decorate the cakes, use shop-bought edible decorations or make Halloween-themed shapes out of sugarpaste (see page 246).

CARDAMOM LOAF

A simple but exotically spiced loaf, perfect with a cup of herbal tea.

Serves 8–10

190g (7oz) unsalted butter,
 softened, plus extra
 for greasing
190g (7oz) plain flour,
 plus extra for dusting
10 cardamom pods, split,
 seeds removed and crushed
 using a pestle and mortar
190g (7oz) caster sugar
3 large eggs
1 tsp baking powder
¼ tsp salt
25ml (1fl oz) soured cream
1 tsp vanilla essence

*One 8.5 x 17.5cm (3½ x 7in)
loaf tin with 7.5cm (3in) sides*

1. Preheat the oven to 170°C (325°F), Gas mark 3, then grease the loaf tin with butter and dust with flour.
2. Using a hand-held electric whisk or a freestanding electric mixer with the paddle attachment, cream together the butter, crushed cardamom seeds and sugar until the mixture is light and fluffy. Break in the eggs one at a time, mixing well after adding each egg. Scrape down the sides of the bowl to make sure all the ingredients are mixed together properly.
3. Sift together the flour, baking powder and salt, then add to the batter, half at a time, and mix together until just incorporated. Finally, mix in the soured cream and vanilla essence.
4. Pour the batter into the prepared loaf tin and bake for 50–60 minutes or until the sponge is firm and a skewer inserted into the middle of the cake comes out clean. Allow the loaf to cool a little before turning it out of the tin on to a wire rack to cool completely, then cutting into slices to serve.

S'MOREANNE CUPCAKES

Our great friend Anne is very talented at inventing new cupcakes. We loved her idea for a s'more-inspired cupcake, so we've named it after her! A s'more is an American campfire treat: marshmallow and chocolate sandwiched between crackers and roasted.

Makes 12–16 cupcakes

FOR THE SPONGE

30g (1oz) dark chocolate (minimum 70% cocoa solids), chilled

5 digestive biscuits

80g (3oz) unsalted butter, softened

280g (10oz) caster sugar

200g (7oz) plain flour

40g (1½oz) cocoa powder

1 tbsp baking powder

¼ tsp salt

2 large eggs

240ml (8½fl oz) whole milk

FOR THE TOPPING

200g (7oz) caster sugar

4 egg whites

100g (3½oz) dark chocolate (minimum 70% cocoa solids), broken into squares, to decorate

One or two 12-hole deep muffin tins
Cook's blowtorch (optional)

1. Preheat the oven to 170°C (325°F), Gas mark 3, and line a muffin tin with muffin cases. Use the finest blade of a cheese grater to shave the chilled chocolate, then set aside. Crush the biscuits in a food processor with the blade attachment or in a plastic bag using a rolling pin.

2. Using a hand-held electric whisk or a freestanding electric mixer with paddle attachment, beat together the butter, sugar, flour, cocoa powder, baking powder and salt on a low speed until resembling fine breadcrumbs.

3. Mix the eggs and milk by hand in a jug, then pour three-quarters of this into the dry ingredients and mix on a low speed to combine. Increase the speed to medium and mix until smooth and thick. Scrape the sides of the bowl, add the remaining milk mixture and keep mixing until all the ingredients are incorporated and the batter is smooth.

4. Fill each paper case two-thirds full with batter. Any remaining batter can be used to fill more cases in a second muffin tin. Sprinkle the chocolate shavings and three-quarters of the crushed biscuits on top of the cupcakes, reserving the remaining biscuit crumbs for later.

5. Bake in the oven for 18–20 minutes or until risen and springy to the touch. Leave to cool slightly, then remove from the tin and place on a wire rack to cool completely before frosting.

6. Put the sugar into a small saucepan with 150ml (5½fl oz) of water and bring to the boil. Meanwhile, using the electric whisk or freestanding mixer with the paddle attachment, whisk the egg whites until foamy.

7. When the sugar has boiled for 5–10 minutes and reached the soft-ball stage (see tip on page 108), pour on to the beaten eggs while mixing on a medium speed (take great care as the sugar will be very hot!) Once added, adjust the speed to high and whisk until the underside of the bowl feels lukewarm. At this stage, the meringue should have increased in size and become white, smooth and quite shiny.

8. Smooth the meringue on to the cooled cupcakes, then swirl or mould into decorative spikes and waves using a palette knife. With a cook's blowtorch, lightly brown the meringue to give it a baked appearance. Alternatively, pop the cakes under a hot grill – but only for a few seconds, as the meringue will brown quickly and you don't want it to burn. Decorate the cupcakes with biscuit crumbs and squares of chocolate.

PUMPKIN, CHEESE AND CHIVE MUFFINS

We love our savoury muffins still warm in the mornings. As with other pumpkin recipes, adding pumpkin purée to these muffins makes them really moist. You can use another sharp cheese instead of Cheddar if you prefer.

Makes 10–12 muffins

60g (2oz) peeled and
   finely chopped onion
½ tsp dried mixed herbs
90g (3oz) unsalted butter
300g (10½oz) plain flour
1 tbsp baking powder
½ tsp bicarbonate of soda
⅛ tsp salt
250ml (9fl oz) whole milk
2 large eggs
50g (1¾oz) tinned pumpkin
   purée
80g (3oz) mature Cheddar
   cheese, grated
30g (1oz) chives, finely
   chopped

One 12-hole deep muffin tin

1. Preheat the oven to 170°C (325°F), Gas mark 3, and line the tin with muffin cases.
2. In a small frying pan over a medium heat, fry the onion together with the mixed herbs in 5g (¼oz) of the butter for 3–4 minutes or until the onions are soft and glossy but not browned. Set aside to cool for a few minutes.
3. Sift together the flour, baking powder, bicarbonate of soda and salt in a large bowl or the bowl of a freestanding electric mixer. In a jug, mix together the milk and eggs. Make a well in the centre of the dry ingredients and pour in the milk and eggs while mixing on a low speed with a hand-held electric whisk or using the mixer with the paddle attachment.
4. Melt the remaining butter in a saucepan over a low heat, then, when all of the other ingredients have come together, pour in the melted butter. Add the pumpkin purée and mix thoroughly. Scrape down the sides of the bowl, and then mix on a medium speed until the batter is smooth. Finally, stir in the grated cheese, chives and cooked onions by hand.
5. Spoon the batter into the paper cases, filling them two-thirds full, then bake for approximately 35 minutes or until the muffins bounce back when lightly touched. Leave in the tin to cool for a little, then transfer to a wire rack.

PUMPKIN CHEESECAKE

A simple-to-make treat for Halloween and the autumn season.

Serves 8–10

FOR THE BISCUIT BASE
220g (8oz) digestive biscuits
100g (3½oz) unsalted butter,
   melted
½ tsp ground cinnamon
½ tsp ground nutmeg

FOR THE CHEESECAKE TOPPING
700g (1½lb) full-fat cream
   cheese (such as Philadelphia)
120g (4oz) caster sugar
1 tsp ground cinnamon
3 large eggs
150g (5½oz) tinned
   pumpkin purée

One 20cm (8in) diameter
spring-form cake tin

1. Line the base of the cake tin with baking parchment, then crush the digestive biscuits into fine crumbs, either in a food processor, with the blade attachment, or in a sealed plastic bag and using a rolling pin.

2. Place the biscuit crumbs in a bowl and mix together with the melted butter. Stir in the ground cinnamon and nutmeg, then pour the buttery mixture into the lined cake tin, pressing it into the base of the tin. Leave in the fridge to cool and set for 20–30 minutes.

3. Meanwhile, preheat the oven to 160°C (320°F), Gas mark 3, and make the cheesecake topping.

4. Using a hand-held electric whisk or a freestanding electric mixer with the paddle attachment, cream together the cream cheese, sugar and cinnamon until smooth. Add the eggs one at a time, mixing each one in thoroughly and scraping down the sides of the bowl before adding the next egg. Stir in the pumpkin and then pour the cheesecake mixture on to the prepared base.

5. Place the cake tin (wrapped in foil, if you like – see the tip on page 80) in a roasting tin and fill with water to about 5mm (¼in) from the top of the cake tin, creating a water bath for the cheesecake to bake in. Carefully place in the oven and bake for 35–45 minutes or until the cheesecake is a light golden colour all over and a little darker around the edges. It should feel firm to the touch with only a slight wobble in the centre.

6. Allow the cheesecake to cool down at room temperature, and then place in the fridge to set for a few hours, or preferably overnight. Carefully remove from the cake tin before serving.

CORNBREAD MUFFINS

Cornbread is a quintessentially American food and easily adapted into these muffins. You can serve them slightly warm with a small knob of butter melting into the yellow cornbread. Perfect for warming up a chilly Bonfire Night.

Makes 10–12 muffins

200g (7oz) fine yellow
   cornmeal
170g (6oz) plain flour
1 tsp baking powder
½ tsp bicarbonate of soda
¾ tsp salt
¼ tsp ground cumin
2 large eggs
350ml (12fl oz) buttermilk
45g (1½oz) unsalted butter,
   melted
3 tbsp runny honey
40g (1½oz) pickled peppers,
   chopped
300g (10½oz) mature Cheddar
   cheese, grated

One 12-hole deep muffin tin

1. Preheat the oven to 190°C (375°F), Gas mark 5, and line the tin with muffin cases.
2. In a large bowl or the bowl of a freestanding electric mixer, mix together the cornmeal, flour, baking powder, bicarbonate of soda, salt and cumin. Break the eggs into a jug and mix together with the buttermilk, melted butter and honey.
3. Make a well in the dry ingredients, then pour in the liquid mixture while mixing on a low speed, using either a hand-held electric whisk or the mixer with the paddle attachment. Once the ingredients have all come together, scrape down the sides of the bowl and mix on a medium speed until the batter is smooth.
4. Add the chopped peppers and 240g (8½oz) of the grated cheese and stir in by hand. Spoon the muffin batter into the paper cases, filling them two-thirds full, and sprinkle the remaining cheese on top.
5. Place in the oven and bake for 25–30 minutes or until the tops of the muffins bounce back when lightly pressed. Allow to cool in the tin for a few minutes, then place on a wire rack to finish cooling.

CHRISTMAS

CHRISTMAS CUPCAKES

This isn't our usual light, moist sponge, but a denser, Christmas-cake version. Enthusiastic bakers can of course soak their mixed dried fruits in rum for longer than the 30 minutes specified in the recipe! Decorate with your favourite edible decorations, which can be bought online, in supermarkets or made by hand (see page 246).

Makes 12–16 cupcakes

FOR THE SPONGE
300g (10½oz) mixed dried fruit
100ml (3½fl oz) rum
200g (7oz) unsalted butter,
   softened
200g (7oz) soft dark
   brown sugar
4 large eggs
160g (5½oz) plain flour
½ tsp baking powder
½ tsp mixed spice
60g (2oz) ground almonds

FOR THE FROSTING
500g (1lb 2oz) icing sugar
160g (5½oz) unsalted butter,
   softened
50ml (1¾fl oz) whole milk
½ tsp almond essence
Red sprinkles, silver balls or
   edible glitter, to decorate
   (optional)

*One or two 12-hole
deep muffin tins*

1. First place the dried fruit in a bowl, pour in the rum and leave to soak for 30 minutes.
2. In the meantime, preheat the oven to 190°C (375°F), Gas mark 5, and line a tin with muffin cases.
3. Using a hand-held electric whisk or a freestanding electric mixer with the paddle attachment, cream together the butter and sugar until light and fluffy. Break in the eggs one at a time, scraping down the sides of the bowl after adding each egg and mixing on a medium speed.
4. Sift together the flour, baking powder and mixed spice, then add to the creamed mixture and whisk on a low speed until all the ingredients are incorporated. Add the ground almonds, followed by the rum-soaked dried fruit, and mix until combined.
5. Divide the batter between the paper cases, filling each two-thirds full. Any remaining batter can be used to fill one to four more cases in another tin. Pop in the oven and bake for 18–20 minutes or until the cupcakes have risen and spring back when you gently press them. Let them cool in the tray for a short while, then transfer to a wire rack to cool completely while you make the frosting.
6. Using the electric whisk or freestanding mixer with the paddle attachment, whisk the icing sugar with the butter on a low speed until fully combined and the mixture is still powdery in texture. Gradually add the milk and, once this has been incorporated, increase the speed to high and whisk until light and fluffy. Add the almond essence and continue to whisk until it is well mixed in.
7. Spoon the frosting on to the cold cupcakes, smoothing it with a palette knife and swirling to finish. For a festive touch, you could add some red sprinkles, edible Christmas-themed shapes, silver sugar balls or a sprinkling of edible glitter.

CHOCOLATE, CARAMEL AND HAZELNUT CHEESECAKE

These three ingredients blend so nicely together and produce a very rich and creamy cheesecake – perfect as a winter dessert.

Serves 8–12

FOR THE BISCUIT BASE
220g (8oz) digestive biscuits
100g (3½oz) unsalted butter,
  melted

FOR THE CHEESECAKE TOPPING
700g (1½lb) full-fat cream
  cheese (such as Philadelphia)
120g (4½oz) caster sugar
3 eggs
50g (1¾oz) tinned caramel
  or *dulce de leche*
50g (1¾oz) dark chocolate
  (minimum 70% cocoa solids),
  broken into pieces

TO FINISH
4 tbsp tinned caramel or
  dulce de leche
2 tbsp chopped hazelnuts,
  roasted (see the tip on
  page 63)

*One 20cm (8in) diameter
spring-form cake tin*

1. Line the base of the cake tin with baking parchment, then whiz the digestive biscuits into fine crumbs in a food processor with the blade attachment. Alternatively, place the biscuits in a plastic bag, seal it shut and crush with a rolling pin.

2. Pour the biscuit crumbs into a bowl, add the melted butter and stir together. Tip the mixture into the lined cake tin, pressing it into the base of the tin, then place in the fridge to chill and set for 20–30 minutes.

3. Meanwhile, preheat the oven to 160°C (320°F), Gas mark 3, and make the cheesecake topping.

4. Using a hand-held electric whisk or a freestanding electric mixer with the paddle attachment, cream together the cream cheese and sugar until smooth. Add the eggs one at a time, mixing thoroughly on a medium speed after each addition and scraping down the sides of the bowl.

5. Transfer a third of the cheesecake mixture to a separate bowl and set aside, then stir the tinned caramel into the remaining cheesecake mix and pour or spoon it on to the prepared biscuit base.

6. In a glass or metal bowl set over a pan of simmering water, gently melt the chocolate. Once it has melted, allow it to cool slightly, then stir into the reserved cheesecake mixture. Spoon the chocolate cheesecake topping on to the caramel mixture in the tin and smooth the top with a spoon.

7. Wrap the cake tin in foil (see the tip on page 80) and place in a roasting tin, filling this with water to about 5mm (¼in) from the top of the cake tin to create a water bath for the cheesecake to bake in, to prevent the top cracking during cooking. Place in the oven and bake for 35–45 minutes or until the cheesecake is a light golden colour (darker around the edges), firm to the touch and with only a slight wobble in the middle.

8. Allow the cheesecake, still in the tin, to cool down to room temperature, and then place in the fridge to set for a few hours, or preferably overnight.

9. Remove the chilled cheesecake from the spring-form tin, then top with the caramel, smoothing it out with a palette knife, and sprinkle over the hazelnuts to decorate.

These have a refreshing minty taste, just like candy-canes for decorating a Christmas tree. With their red-and-white striped frosting, these cupcakes make great festive gifts. They are sprinkled with transparent sugar, which can be bought online or from specialist cake shops.

Makes 12–16 cupcakes

FOR THE SPONGE

80g (3oz) unsalted butter, softened
280g (10oz) caster sugar
240g (8½oz) plain flour
1 tbsp baking powder
¼ tsp salt
240ml (8½fl oz) whole milk
1 tsp vanilla essence
2 large eggs

FOR THE FROSTING

500g (1lb 2oz) icing sugar
160g (5½oz) unsalted butter, softened
4 tsp peppermint essence
50ml (1¾fl oz) whole milk
¼ tsp Christmas-red food-colouring paste or 2–3 tsp liquid food colouring (such as Dr Oetker)
Transparent sugar, for sprinkling

One or two 12-hole deep muffin tins
Piping bag with a medium-sized (no. 7 or 8) nozzle

1. Preheat the oven to 190°C (375°F), Gas mark 5, and line a muffin tin with muffin cases.

2. Using a hand-held electric whisk or a freestanding electric mixer with the paddle attachment, slowly whisk together the butter, sugar, flour, baking powder and salt until the mixture resembles fine breadcrumbs.

3. Place the milk in a jug with the vanilla essence, add the eggs and whisk together by hand. Pour three-quarters of the whisked milk and eggs into the dry ingredients and mix on a low speed to combine. Increase the speed to medium and continue to mix until smooth and thick. Scrape down the sides of the bowl, add the remaining milk mixture and keep mixing on a medium speed until all the ingredients are incorporated and the batter is smooth once again.

4. Spoon the batter into the muffin cases, filling each one up to two-thirds. If any batter is left, use it to fill up to four more cases in another tin. Bake in the oven for 18–20 minutes or until well risen and springy to the touch. Leave to cool in the tray for a few minutes, then place on a wire rack to cool completely before you add the frosting.

5. Using the electric whisk or the freestanding mixer with the paddle attachment, beat the icing sugar with the butter and peppermint essence on a low speed until the mixture is sandy in consistency, with no large lumps of butter left in the bowl.

6. Gradually add the milk and slowly mix until incorporated, then increase the speed to high and whisk until light and fluffy. Divide the frosting into two, leaving one as it is and mixing the food colouring into the second batch.

7. Fill the piping bag with half red and half white frosting. The two colours should be next to each other, not one above the other, so that you pipe them out into a red and white line of frosting, like a striped candy cane. Pipe the frosting in an ice cream-type swirl on top of each cake and then sprinkle with transparent sugar.

SNICKERDOODLE COOKIES

Crunchy and cinnamony, these cookies can be wrapped in parchment paper, tied with ribbon and given as a delicious edible Christmas present.

Makes 14–18 cookies

FOR THE DOUGH
60g (2oz) unsalted butter, softened
160g (5½oz) caster sugar
¼ tsp vanilla essence
1 large egg
240g (8½oz) plain flour
¾ tsp cream of tartar
½ tsp bicarbonate of soda
⅛ tsp salt
¼ tsp ground cinnamon

FOR THE COATING
1½ tbsp caster sugar
1 tbsp ground cinnamon

1. Using a hand-held electric whisk or a freestanding electric mixer with the paddle attachment, cream together the butter, sugar and vanilla essence until light and fluffy. Add the egg and mix well, scraping down the sides of the bowl to make sure all the ingredients are fully incorporated.
2. Sift together the remaining ingredients and add these to the creamed mixture in two or three batches. Mix well using the mixer or by hand until the dough forms a smooth ball. Place the dough in a bowl, cover with cling film and place in the fridge to chill and rest for approximately 40 minutes.
3. While the dough is resting, preheat the oven to 170°C (325°F), Gas mark 3, and line two to three baking sheets with baking parchment.
4. Next mix together the caster sugar and ground cinnamon for the coating in a small bowl.
5. Once the dough is ready, break off small, walnut-sized pieces of the dough and roll these in the cinnamon sugar, making sure each ball is completely coated. Place the dough balls on to the prepared baking sheets, allowing five or six cookies per sheet and arranging them 4–5cm (1½–2in) apart to give them space to spread during cooking.
6. Pop in the oven and bake for 10–13 minutes or until the cookies are a light golden colour. Allow to cool and set on the sheets for a few minutes before removing to a wire rack.

EGGNOG CUPCAKES

Full of Christmas flavours, with rum and nutmeg-flavoured frosting on a light, airy sponge. Sprinkle with grated nutmeg, or decorate with edible Christmas decorations.

Makes 12–16 cupcakes

FOR THE SPONGE
80g (3oz) unsalted butter, softened
280g (10oz) caster sugar
240g (8½oz) plain flour
1 tbsp baking powder
¼ tsp salt
2 large eggs
240ml (8½fl oz) milk

FOR THE FROSTING
500g (1lb 2oz) icing sugar
160g (5½oz) unsalted butter, softened
2 tsp rum essence
1 tsp freshly grated nutmeg
50ml (1¾fl oz) whole milk
Edible Christmas-themed shapes, to decorate

One or two 12-hole deep muffin tins

1. Preheat the oven to 190°C (375°F), Gas mark 5, and fill a muffin tin with muffin cases.
2. Using a hand-held electric whisk or freestanding electric mixer with the paddle attachment, beat together the butter, sugar, flour, baking powder and salt on a low speed until they have the texture of fine breadcrumbs.
3. Break the eggs into a jug, add the milk and whisk by hand, then pour three-quarters of this mixture into the dry ingredients and mix on a low speed to combine. Increase the speed to medium and keep mixing until smooth and thick. Scrape down the sides of the bowl, add the remaining milk mixture and continue beating on a medium speed until all the ingredients are mixed in and the batter is smooth.
4. Fill the paper cases two-thirds full with the batter. If any remains, it can be used to fill up to four more cases in a second muffin tin. Bake in the oven for 18–20 minutes or until risen and springy to the touch. Leave in the tray for a few minutes, then transfer to a wire rack to cool completely before adding the frosting.
5. Using the electric whisk or freestanding mixer with the paddle attachment, whisk the icing sugar with the butter, rum essence and grated nutmeg on a low speed until no large lumps of butter are left and the mixture is crumbly. Gradually add the milk, then increase the speed to high and whisk until light and fluffy.
6. Once the cupcakes are cold to the touch, smooth the frosting on top of each cake using a palette knife and add a decorative swirl. Decorate with shop-bought edible Christmas-themed shapes, or make your own from sugarpaste (see page 246).

WHITE CHOCOLATE AND CRANBERRY COOKIES

Slightly tart cranberries and sweet white chocolate chips make a great taste combination that is perfectly suited to the festive season. If you like your cookies a bit soft and chewy, then take them out of the oven as soon as they start to turn golden.

Makes 10–12 cookies

135g (5oz) unsalted butter
80g (3oz) caster sugar
80g (3oz) soft light
   brown sugar
1 egg
½ tsp vanilla essence
190g (7oz) plain flour
½ tsp salt
¼ tsp ground cinnamon
½ tsp bicarbonate of soda
100g (3½oz) dried cranberries
60g (2oz) white chocolate chips

1. Preheat the oven to 170°C (325°F), Gas mark 3, and line two baking sheets with baking parchment.
2. Using a hand-held electric whisk or a freestanding electric mixer with the paddle attachment, cream together the butter and both types of sugar, then break in the egg, add the vanilla essence and mix well together.
3. Sift together the flour, salt, cinnamon and bicarbonate of soda, then add to the creamed mixture in two batches, mixing thoroughly in the mixer or by hand until a dough forms. Lastly stir in the cranberries and chocolate chips.
4. Break off pieces of the dough (about 2 tablespoons in size), roll them into balls and place on the prepared baking sheets. Allow five or six cookies per tray, making sure to space them apart from each other (by 7–8cm/about 3in) as they will spread during cooking.
5. Place in the oven and bake for 15-20 minutes or until the cookies are a light golden on top. Leave on the sheets for about 10 minutes to cool and set before transferring to a wire rack.

CHOCOLATE AND LIME CHEESECAKE

Lime is such a wonderful citrus fruit, tangy yet fragrant, giving this cheesecake the perfect lift. We like to decorate this simply with chocolate shavings and grated lime zest.

Serves 8–12

FOR THE BISCUIT BASE
250g (9oz) double-chocolate cookies
100g (3½oz) unsalted butter, melted

FOR THE CHEESECAKE TOPPING
800g (1¾lb) full-fat cream cheese (such as Philadelphia)
150g (5½oz) caster sugar
3 large eggs
Zest and juice of 6 limes, plus zest of 1 extra lime, to decorate
20g (¾oz) dark chocolate, grated

One 20cm (8in) diameter spring-form cake tin

1. First line the cake tin with baking parchment, then blitz the cookies into a rough crumb in a food processor with the blade attachment. If you prefer, place the biscuits in a plastic bag, seal it shut and crush with a rolling pin.
2. Tip the cookie crumbs into a bowl, add the melted butter and mix together with a spoon. Pour the mixture into the prepared cake tin, pressing the crumbs down firmly into the base of the tin using the spoon, then place in the fridge to chill and set for 20–30 minutes.
3. In the meantime, preheat the oven to 160°C (320°F), Gas mark 3, and make the cheesecake topping.
4. Using a hand-held electric whisk or a freestanding electric mixer with the paddle attachment, mix the cream cheese on a medium speed until smooth. Add the sugar and beat until combined, then break in the eggs one at a time, mixing well after each egg. Scrape down the sides of the bowl after each addition to make sure all the ingredients are evenly incorporated. Lastly, add the lime juice and zest and mix in well.
5. Pour the cream cheese mixture on to the set cookie base, then wrap the cake tin in foil (see the tip on page 80) and place in a roasting tin filled with water up to about 5mm (¼in) from the top of the cake tin. This helps prevent the cheesecake from drying out as it cooks.
6. Place the cheesecake in the oven and bake for 30–40 minutes or until it has set and has only a very slight wobble in the centre. Allow it to cool slightly while in the roasting tin, then remove from the water and allow to cool to room temperature before placing in the fridge for a few hours, or preferably overnight. Remove the spring-form tin before serving. Sprinkle with grated lime zest and dark chocolate to decorate.

CINNAMON AND RAISIN LOAF

This loaf looks great when sliced. Soured cream keeps the sponge so moist and, if you prefer, you can substitute currants or mixed dried fruits for the raisins.

Serves 8–10

190g (7oz) unsalted butter, softened, plus extra for greasing

190g (7oz) plain flour, plus extra for dusting

190g (7oz) caster sugar

3 eggs

1 tsp baking powder

¼ tsp salt

25ml (1fl oz) soured cream

1 tsp vanilla essence

1 tbsp ground cinnamon

70g (2½oz) raisins

One 8.5 x 17.5cm (3½ x 7in) loaf tin with 7.5cm (3in) sides

1. Preheat the oven to 170°C (325°F), Gas mark 3, then grease the loaf tin with butter and dust with flour.
2. Using a hand-held electric whisk or a freestanding electric mixer with the paddle attachment, cream together the butter and sugar until pale and fluffy. Break the eggs in one at a time, mixing well after each addition and scraping down the sides of the bowl to make sure all the ingredients are fully incorporated.
3. Sift together the flour, baking powder and salt, then add to the batter in two batches and mix on a low speed until just incorporated. Finally, mix in the soured cream and vanilla essence.
4. Spoon about 200g (7oz) of the batter into a small bowl and stir in the cinnamon. Stir the raisins into the remaining batter, then pour this batter into the prepared loaf tin. Spoon the cinnamon batter on top and swirl the two together for a marbled effect.
5. Bake the loaf in the oven for 50–60 minutes or until the sponge feels firm on top and a skewer inserted into the centre of the loaf comes out clean of any uncooked batter. Allow the loaf to cool a little before turning it out of the tin on to a wire rack to cool completely before you serve it.

RED VELVET WHOOPIE PIES

We just had to make our bestselling cupcake flavour into a whoopie pie! The contrast of red and white looks just wonderful for Christmas, but of course they are tasty any time of the year.

Makes 8–10 pies

FOR THE SPONGE

120g (4½oz) unsalted butter, softened

200g (7oz) soft dark brown sugar

1 large egg

120ml (4fl oz) buttermilk

1 tsp vanilla essence

340g (12oz) plain flour

2 tbsp cocoa powder

½ tsp bicarbonate of soda

¼ tsp salt

30ml (1fl oz) red food colouring (such as Dr Oetker)

FOR THE FILLING

85g (3oz) unsalted butter, softened

150g (5½oz) icing sugar

80g (3oz) full-fat cream cheese (such as Philadelphia)

100g (3½oz) vanilla Marshmallow Fluff

1. Preheat the oven to 170°C (325°F), Gas mark 3, and line two baking trays with baking parchment.

2. Using a hand-held electric whisk or freestanding electric mixer with the paddle attachment, cream the butter and sugar together until light and fluffy. Add the egg and mix in thoroughly, scraping down the sides of the bowl.

3. In a jug mix together the buttermilk and vanilla essence by hand, then add on a low speed to the creamed mixture. Sift together the flour, cocoa powder, bicarbonate of soda and salt and add to the batter in two batches, mixing thoroughly after each addition until all the ingredients have come together. Add the red food colouring, then increase the speed to medium-to-high and mix together well to ensure the batter is an even red colour. Leave the batter in the fridge for 20–30 minutes to cool and set slightly.

4. Spoon the batter on to the prepared trays, making eight to ten mounds per tray, each 3–5cm (1¼–2in) in diameter and 2–3 cm (¾–1¼in) apart. Bake in the oven for 10–13 minutes or until springy to the touch, then allow to cool completely before you assemble the pies.

5. While the sponges are cooking, make the filling. Using a hand-held electric whisk or freestanding electric mixer with the paddle attachment, mix together the butter and icing sugar on a low speed until combined. Add the cream cheese and mix in, still on a low speed. Once all the ingredients are mixed, increase the speed to high and beat for approximately 1 minute.

6. Add the marshmallow fluff and beat the filling, still on a high speed, until it is light and fluffy, then place the filling in the fridge for about 30 minutes to firm up slightly.

7. When the cakes have cooled down, spread about 1 tablespoon of the filling on the flat side of one of the sponges, adding a little more if needed. Then stick another sponge (flat side down) on top to make a sandwich, and repeat with the remaining sponges and filling.

LEMON AND CRANBERRY CUPCAKES

Cranberries go with more than just the Christmas turkey. In these cupcakes, cranberry and lemon add a tart edge to the sweet frosting.

Makes 12–16 cupcakes

FOR THE SPONGE
80g (3oz) unsalted butter, softened
280g (10oz) caster sugar
240g (8½oz) plain flour
1 tbsp baking powder
¼ tsp salt
1½ tsp finely grated lemon zest
240ml (8½fl oz) whole milk
2 large eggs
1½ tsp vanilla essence
100g (3½oz) dried cranberries, chopped

FOR THE FROSTING
500g (1lb 2oz) icing sugar
160g (5½oz) unsalted butter, softened
50ml (1¾fl oz) whole milk
1 tsp finely grated lemon zest
100g (3½oz) dried cranberries, chopped (optional)

One or two 12-hole deep muffin tins

1. Preheat the oven to 190°C (375°F), Gas mark 5, and line a tin with muffin cases.
2. Using a hand-held electric whisk or freestanding electric mixer with the paddle attachment, beat together the butter, sugar, flour, baking powder, salt and lemon zest on a low speed until they resemble fine breadcrumbs.
3. Place the milk, eggs and vanilla essence in a jug and whisk by hand until combined. Pour three-quarters of this mixture into the dry ingredients and mix together on a low speed. Increase the speed to medium and keep mixing until smooth and thick. Scrape down the sides of the bowl, add the remaining milk mixture and continue to beat until all the ingredients have been mixed in and the batter is smooth once again. Stir in the dried cranberries by hand.
4. Fill each muffin case up to two-thirds full with the batter. If any remains, use it to fill up to four more cases in a second tin. Bake for 18–20 minutes or until the cupcakes are risen and spring back when lightly pressed. Leave them in the tin to cool a little, then transfer to a wire rack to cool completely before adding the frosting.
5. Using the electric whisk or freestanding electric mixer with the paddle attachment, whisk the icing sugar with the butter on a low speed until sandy-textured and no large lumps of butter remain. Gradually mix in the milk, then increase the speed to high and whisk until soft and light. Add the lemon zest and cranberries, if using, and continue to mix for a further 30 seconds until combined.
6. Divide the frosting between the cold cupcakes, using a palette knife to smooth it on and make a swirl on top of each cake.

HONEY AND PEAR LAYER CAKE

A delightful cake for a special occasion, the caramelised pears in this recipe are divine. Just make sure you don't overcook them or they may become too soft and mushy.

Serves 14–16

FOR THE CARAMELISED PEARS
3 pears
20g (¾oz) unsalted butter
60g (2oz) runny honey
40g (1½oz) caster sugar

FOR THE SPONGE
4 large eggs
120g (4oz) caster sugar
40g (1½oz) soft light
  brown sugar
120ml (4fl oz) buttermilk
120g (4oz) runny honey
120ml (4fl oz) vegetable oil
1 tsp finely grated lemon zest
280g (10oz) plain flour
1½ tsp baking powder
1 tsp bicarbonate of soda
1 tsp ground cinnamon
1 tsp salt

FOR THE FROSTING
500g (1lb 2oz) icing sugar
100g (3½oz) unsalted butter,
  softened
250g (9oz) full-fat cream cheese
  (such as Philadelphia)
50g (1¾oz) runny honey
Ground cinnamon, for dusting
  (optional)

Four 20cm (8in) diameter loose-bottomed sandwich tins

1. Preheat the oven to 170°C (325°F), Gas mark 3, and line the base of the sandwich tins with baking parchment.
2. First cook the pears. Peel and core the fruit and cut each lengthways into about 12 slices. Place the remaining ingredients in a saucepan and melt together over a low heat. Add the sliced pears and cook until the fruit is soft and golden. Set aside to cool while you make the sponge batter.
3. Using a hand-held electric whisk or a freestanding electric mixer with the paddle attachment, cream together the eggs and both types of sugars until light and fluffy. In a jug stir together the buttermilk, honey, vegetable oil and lemon zest. Pour this liquid mixture into the creamed ingredients while mixing on a low speed.
4. Sift together the remaining ingredients, add to the creamed mixture and mix together on a medium speed to ensure everything is well incorporated.
5. Divide the cake batter evenly between the prepared cake tins. Top the batter with the cooked pears, allowing nine slices per cake and placing them in concentric circles, each slice spaced evenly apart.
6. Place in the oven and bake for 25–30 minutes or until each sponge is golden brown on top and bounces back when lightly pressed. Allow the cakes to cool completely, on a wire rack, before you frost them.
7. Using the electric whisk or mixer with the paddle attachment, slowly mix the butter and icing sugar together until no large lumps of butter remain and the ingredients have a sandy consistency. Add the cream cheese and honey and continue mixing on a low speed until incorporated, then increase the speed to medium and beat the frosting until it is light and fluffy.
8. Once the sponges have cooled, place the first layer on a plate or cake card and top with 3–4 tablespoons of the honey frosting, smoothing it on with a palette knife and adding a little more if needed. Continue this process, adding the second layer of sponge and topping with frosting. Repeat with the third layer, then add the final sponge and frost the sides and top of the cake, covering it completely so that no sponge can be seen.
9. Decorate the cake with crystallised fruits (see page 248) and a light dusting of ground cinnamon if you like.

PISTACHIO LOAF

The lovely green colour of ground pistachios really stands out against the white glaze on this moist and delicious loaf.

Serves 8–10

FOR THE SPONGE

190g (7oz) unsalted butter,
  softened, plus extra
  for greasing
190g (7oz) plain flour,
  plus extra for dusting
190g (7oz) caster sugar
3 large eggs
1 tsp baking powder
¼ tsp salt
25ml (1fl oz) soured cream
1 tsp vanilla essence
100g (3½oz) shelled pistachios,
  roughly chopped

FOR THE GLAZE

120g (4oz) icing sugar
40g (1½oz) ground pistachios
  (see the tip on page 55)

*One 8.5 x 17.5cm (3½ x 7in)
loaf tin with 7.5cm (3in) sides*

1. Preheat the oven to 170°C (325°F), Gas mark 3, then grease the loaf tin with butter and dust with flour.

2. Using a hand-held electric whisk or a freestanding electric mixer with the paddle attachment, cream together the butter and sugar until pale and fluffy. Add the eggs one at a time, mixing well after each addition and scraping down the sides of the bowl to make sure all the ingredients are properly mixed together.

3. Sift together the flour, baking powder and salt, then add to the creamed mixture in two batches and mix on a low speed until just incorporated. Add the soured cream and vanilla essence, then stir in the chopped pistachios by hand.

4. Pour or spoon the batter into the prepared tin, then place in the oven and bake for 50–60 minutes or until the sponge feels firm to the touch and a skewer inserted into the middle of the loaf comes out clean, with no uncooked batter sticking to it.

5. Allow the loaf to cool a little in the tin, then turn out on to a wire rack to cool down fully before adding the glaze.

6. Place the icing sugar in a bowl, add 2 tablespoons of water and mix together. This will form a fairly runny paste; if the glaze seems too thick, add a little more water to thin it – ¼ teaspoon at a time. Stir in the ground pistachios, keeping a small amount aside to sprinkle on top. Pour the glaze over the cooled loaf and sprinkle with the remaining pistachios.

GINGERBREAD CUPCAKES

Black treacle, golden syrup and rich, warm spices really make these cupcakes taste like traditional Christmas gingerbread. The lemony cream-cheese frosting is perfect with the spicy sponge.

Makes 12–16 cupcakes

FOR THE SPONGE
140g (5oz) unsalted butter, softened
200g (7oz) caster sugar
60g (2oz) black treacle
60g (2oz) golden syrup
2 large eggs
2 large egg yolks
310g (11oz) plain flour
1 tbsp cocoa powder
1 tsp ground ginger
1 tsp ground cinnamon
1 tsp ground nutmeg
2 tsp baking powder
1 tsp salt
240ml (8½fl oz) hot milk

FOR THE FROSTING
600g (1lb 5oz) icing sugar
100g (3½oz) unsalted butter, softened
250g (9oz) full-fat cream cheese (such as Philadelphia)
1 tsp finely grated lemon zest
Edible Christmas-themed shapes, to decorate

One or two 12-hole deep muffin tins

1. Preheat the oven to 190°C (375°F), Gas mark 5, and line a muffin tin with muffin cases.
2. Using a hand-held electric whisk or freestanding electric mixer with the paddle attachment, cream the butter and caster sugar together until pale and fluffy. Add the treacle, golden syrup, eggs and egg yolks and continue mixing until all ingredients are evenly combined.
3. Sift together the flour, cocoa powder, spices, baking powder and salt. Add the dry ingredients to the butter and egg mixture, mixing on a low speed and adding in two or three batches, alternating with the hot milk. Continue to mix, on a medium speed, until all the ingredients are well incorporated and the batter is smooth.
4. Divide the batter between the muffin cases, filling each one two-thirds full. Any remaining batter can be used to fill one to four more cases in a separate tin. Pop in the oven and bake for 18–20 minutes or until risen and springy to the touch. Allow to cool in the tin for a short while, then remove to a wire rack to cool down completely while you prepare the frosting.
5. Using the electric whisk or freestanding mixer with the paddle attachment, slowly whisk the icing sugar with the butter until no large lumps of butter remain and the mixture is sandy in consistency. Add the cream cheese and mix on a medium-to-high speed until the frosting is light, fluffy and smooth. Stir in the lemon zest by hand.
6. Divide the frosting between the cold cupcakes, smoothing it on with a palette knife, and add a swirl at the top. If you want to decorate the cakes, add shop-bought edible decorations (we've used mini gingerbread men) or make your own shapes out of sugarpaste (see page 246).

CHOCOLATE ORANGE CUPCAKES

We love eating chocolate oranges at Christmas time, but these cupcakes do the job perfectly. We've indulged and topped them with a special chocolate-orange cream cheese frosting! The candied orange peel on top can be bought; look in sweet shops, online or the gift aisles of larger supermarkets.

Makes 12–16 cupcakes

FOR THE SPONGE

70g (2½oz) unsalted butter, softened
210g (7½oz) caster sugar
105g (3½oz) soft light brown sugar
2 large eggs
1 tsp vanilla essence
1 tbsp finely grated orange zest
255g (9oz) plain flour
50g (1¾oz) cocoa powder
2 tsp baking powder
¼ tsp salt
240ml (8½fl oz) whole milk

FOR THE FROSTING

600g (1lb 5oz) icing sugar
100g (3½oz) unsalted butter, softened
250g (9oz) full-fat cream cheese (such as Philadelphia)
60g (2oz) cocoa powder
3 tsp finely grated orange zest
Candied orange peel, thinly sliced, to decorate

One or two 12-hole deep muffin tins

1. Preheat the oven to 190°C (375°F), Gas mark 5, and fill a muffin tin with muffin cases.
2. Using a hand-held electric whisk or a freestanding electric mixer with the paddle attachment, cream together the butter and both types of sugar until pale and fluffy, then beat in the eggs one at a time on a medium speed, followed by the vanilla essence and orange zest.
3. Sift together the remaining ingredients, then add to the creamed mixture in three batches with the milk, alternating between each and mixing on a low speed. Scrape down the sides of the bowl after each addition, and once everything has been incorporated, raise the speed to medium and continue beating until the batter is well mixed and smooth.
4. Divide the mixture between the paper cases, filling each up to two-thirds full. Any remaining batter can used to fill up to four more cases in a separate tin. Place in the oven and bake for 18–20 minutes or until the sponges spring back when you gently press them. Allow to cool for a short while in the tin, then transfer to a wire rack to cool completely before frosting.
5. To make the frosting, whisk the icing sugar with the butter on a low speed, using either the electric whisk or the freestanding mixer with the paddle attachment, until crumbly in texture and no large lumps of butter remain. Add the cream cheese and cocoa powder and continue to mix, on a medium speed, until the frosting is smooth and light. Add the orange zest and stir in by hand.
6. Divide the frosting between the cold cupcakes, smoothing on with a palette knife and swirling the tops for a decorative finish. Top with slices of candied orange peel.

BAKING ESSENTIALS

Before you get into the kitchen and start baking, take a minute or so to read through some useful advice that will help ensure your homemade cakes are as delicious and lovely as the ones in our shops. Baking is fun and you don't have to be an expert to do it, just get to know the basics, prepare yourself with the right ingredients and equipment, and your Hummingbird cakes will be perfect! Even if you're well-practised at baking, our tips and shortcuts can help save time and make your cakes even better, so read on for some wise words from the Hummingbird bakers.

INGREDIENTS

- The better your ingredients, the better your cakes will look and taste. Buy the best you can afford and try not to skimp on quality.
- Our recipes give quantities and measures in metric and imperial, so that everyone can follow them, no matter what type of equipment or oven they have. Always use the same system throughout a recipe – never mix the two. We recommend a set of digital scales, for measuring exact amounts. It really is essential that your measuring is precise, especially for frosting, else the finished results may not be as good as hoped, or the cakes might not turn out quite like the photographs.
- All spoon measurements are level, unless otherwise stated.
- Butter should always be unsalted, as salt can affect the flavour of the cake. It needs to be very soft, so get it out of the fridge long in advance (or soften for a few seconds in the microwave if necessary).
- When using dairy products like milk, cream or cream cheese, always use the whole or full-fat varieties for best results. For all recipes that require cream cheese, we recommend using full-fat Philadelphia.
- All eggs should be large and at room temperature.
- Use a really good-quality cocoa powder (such as Green & Blacks) and good-quality chocolate with a minimum of 70% cocoa solids.
- Baking powder and bicarbonate of soda have important jobs to do, helping cakes to rise and creating the right texture, so make sure they haven't passed their best-before dates, or they may not be effective. Also, if a recipe calls for plain flour, never substitute self-raising flour, as this contains raising agents and will affect the outcome.
- It's good practice to sift flour, cocoa powder and icing sugar before use. This removes lumps and improves the texture of the finished cake. If combining dry ingredients like these, it is easiest to simply sift them together, then mix them by hand with a spoon (avoid mixing them with

a machine as this raises a dust cloud, sending some of your carefully weighed ingredients up into the air.)

- Nuts are often nice toasted or roasted before use, which really improves their flavour. Simply pop them into a saucepan and toss over a medium-to-high heat for 2–3 minutes. Remove from the heat as soon as they turn brown as they can burn easily.

- There are many brands and types of food colourings; each may give a slightly different final shade to your cake or frosting. Although liquid food colouring is the easiest to get hold of, we recommend a paste, which normally results in a better colour. Pastes are available from cookshops or specialist cake shops. You will need less paste than you would liquid; just add a little at a time until you reach the desired colour.

- While we're on the subject of colour, red is generally the trickiest to achieve. For recipes such as the Red Velvet Cupcakes (see page 178) or Christmas recipes like the Candy-cane Cupcakes (page 208), steer clear of bottles labelled 'natural red' or 'scarlet' as they aren't strong enough to create a good depth of colour. (Adding more doesn't tend to work; it just spoils the flavour and often causes the batter or frosting to split.) The most reliable red liquid colouring is Dr Oetker 'Red', available from Sainsbury's, other supermarkets and online.

- We have tried to ensure that most of the ingredients in our recipes can be bought from supermarkets. However, some of the recipes do call for slightly unusual ingredients, such as Marshmallow Fluff. Many of these are available in larger supermarkets or in specialist cake stores. If you are struggling to locate them, search online for suppliers. We've included a directory of suppliers on page 249, where we suggest stockists for some of the trickier ingredients, so that you never find yourself stuck.

EQUIPMENT

- Baking is a science so it is really important that you measure your ingredients accurately. A set of digital scales is ideal for the most precise measuring.

- Most of our recipes call for either a freestanding electric mixer (with a paddle attachment) or a hand-held electric whisk. It's essential to use one of these; mixing the ingredients by hand is rarely as effective and the finished cake won't be as successful. A hand-held electric whisk (or a hand-held blender with a whisk attachment) can be bought cheaply from larger supermarkets and is a great investment for all types of recipes – baking or other.

- Always use the size of cake tin specified in the recipe. (Using the wrong size will affect the cooking time, the batter may cook unevenly and it could overflow.) No matter what size of tin a particular recipe calls for, as a general rule you should always fill it about two-thirds full.
- For cupcakes and muffins, a deep muffin tin is best (usually with 12 holes). Do try and get a deep one, as regular 'bun tins' are designed for fairy-cake style cakes rather than the generous Hummingbird cupcakes.
- The best cake tins are non-stick, loose-bottomed ones. Even if using non-stick, you should still always grease or line the tin as instructed. This will help stop the cake sticking to the inside of the tin and make it easier to remove, avoiding the edges breaking or crumbling and making the finished cake look gorgeous.
  - For layer cakes, use three or four 20cm (8in) loose-bottomed sandwich tins
  - Cheesecakes are best made in a 20–23cm (8–9in) spring-form tin
  - Tarts and pies normally require a 23cm (9in) loose-bottomed tart tin
  - Bake loaf cakes in standard non-stick loaf tins

- When making bars, slices or pies, you might prefer to use a foil tray or foil pie dishes, instead of a regular metal tin. These are especially good if you want to transport the cakes or give them away as a gift. They are available from Lakeland, specialist cake shops and catering suppliers.
- All the recipes in this book have been tested in a conventional oven. If you are using a fan-assisted oven (which tends to cook things faster) it's a good idea to read the manufacturer's instruction booklet, which will probably recommend turning down the temperature a little. If you no longer have the oven instructions, we suggest reducing the temperature by 10 per cent.
- All ovens vary in temperature and many people have 'slow' ovens without even realising it. An oven thermometer is a very useful piece of equipment. It can be permanently hooked into your oven so you can always be sure you are cooking your cakes at the correct temperature.

METHOD AND TECHNIQUES

- Follow each recipe exactly as written. Baking isn't a time for experimenting; the wrong balance of ingredients can cause a recipe to fail. Our methods may seem unconventional at times, but they are tried and tested, so trust us!
- When creaming butter and sugar, it should be done for a good amount of time – 5 minutes or more – until the mixture is really light and fluffy. It is almost impossible to beat the mixture too much at this stage. However, once the flour is added, beat as little as possible, gently folding or stirring it in until just incorporated, as over-beating the mixture at this point will result in the cake being dense or heavy.
- When adding liquid ingredients to a cake batter, it is usually best to do this in a couple of batches, pouring in just a bit at a time and mixing well between each addition to properly combine the ingredients.
- Our cake batter can be quite runny and may sometimes look a little spilt; don't panic, the cakes will bake beautifully.
- Cooking times can really vary depending upon your oven (and also how many items are baking at the same time). Just because the specified cooking time is up, it doesn't automatically mean the cakes are done. For every recipe, we give a time range, so use this as a rough guide, checking the cakes after the minimum time, but leaving them for longer if they need more time in the oven, and checking them regularly.
- Try to avoid opening the oven door until the minimum recommended cooking time, or you risk your cakes sinking or cheesecakes cracking.
- To tell when cakes, cupcakes or muffins are ready, insert a skewer into the middle. If it comes out clean, with no mixture stuck to it, the cake is cooked. You should also look to see if the cakes are well risen, springy on top and golden brown (though this last bit obviously depends on the flavour or colour of the cake – for example, chocolate sponge will never be golden!)
- When making frosting, don't worry if the proportions seem a little odd or if it takes ages for the butter to incorporate with the icing sugar. It's correct for the mixture to be quite fine and 'sandy'. Once you add the milk, all of a sudden it will begin to come together to make a nice, soft, fluffy icing. It takes a bit longer than conventional butter icing, but the result is much more delicious.
- Cakes should be completely cool before you frost them. Otherwise the frosting might melt or slide off the cake.
- Frosting can be piped or scooped onto cakes (avoid using a spoon as this tends to get messy) and swirled with a palette knife. For the Hummingbird technique, see the step-by-step instructions on pages 240–3.
- All cakes are best kept in an airtight container. If stored like this, layer cakes can last up to 5 days and cupcakes will stay incredibly moist for 2 days.

EXTRA TIPS FOR CUPCAKES AND MUFFINS

- As mentioned, a deep muffin tin is ideal (usually with 12 holes). The deep ones are more suitable than regular 'bun tins', which are designed for fairy-cake style cakes rather than our generous Hummingbird cupcakes.
- For all our cupcake and muffin recipes, we recommend using standard muffin cases. (Note that regular cake cases are too small – you will get fairy cakes, not cupcakes.) Dr Oetker muffin cases are readily available from supermarkets, as are own-brand muffin cases. Don't worry that the muffins and cakes are cooked in the same-sized cases; the nature of muffin batter means that they will rise more, resulting in a 'muffin top'.
- To fill the cases evenly, so that your cupcakes or muffins are uniform in size and height, we suggest using an ice cream scoop to measure an exact quantity of batter each time. You can easily buy a suitable scoop from supermarkets, cookshops or online. The scoop we use holds 50ml (1¾fl oz) of batter, which is just under 4 tablespoons. (Of course, you can measure with a tablespoon instead, but this is more long-winded.) A less accurate method is to simply fill each case three-quarters full.
- The cupcake recipes all make 12–16 cakes, so you may find that you've filled your 12-hole muffin tin and still have some batter left over. If you own a second tin, fill more cases with the remaining batter and cook at the same time. If you have only one tin, set the remaining batter aside in a cool place, wait until the first batch is out of the oven, remove them from the tin, then fill more cases with the remaining batter and cook a second batch.
- The mini cupcake recipes (see pages 146–51) make 24–30 cakes. You can buy 24-hole mini muffin tins, and mini muffin cases are available for lining them. If you have leftover batter once the tin is full, either cook simultaneously in a second tin, or set the batter aside in a cool place until the first batch is out of the oven, then you can re-use the tin for the remaining cakes.
- All cupcakes should be cooked on the middle shelf of the oven for 18–20 minutes (apart from the mini ones, which take 12–15 minutes).

EXTRA TIPS FOR LAYER CAKES, CHEESECAKES AND PIES

- When making a layer cake, you want all the layers to cook and rise evenly. For this, it is best to bake them all on the middle shelf of the oven, so you will probably need to bake in batches, putting two layers in the oven at a time (unless your oven is wide enough to fit more onto the shelf).
- Cheesecakes can be tricky to perfect, because they often crack across the top. A good technique to avoid this is to put the cheesecake tin into a 'bain marie' (a water bath) while it is baking. (A roasting tin is ideal, filled with water to about 5mm (¼in) from the top of the cake tin.) This creates moisture in the oven to prevent the cheesecake from drying out and cracking. If you're worried about the tin leaking and water coming into contact with the mixture, wrap the tin with foil before putting it into the bain marie. Another way to help avoid a cheesecake cracking is to thoroughly grease the tin – the cake shrinks whilst cooking, so it needs to be free to pull away from the sides. Also try not to open the oven door during the cooking time as the blast of cooler air can cause the cheesecake to crack.
- Pies and tarts normally have a pastry base, which needs to be 'blind baked' before adding the filling. To do this, line your tart tin with the pastry and then put it in the fridge to rest for 20–30 minutes. Next, cover it with a sheet of baking parchment and fill with baking beans (or uncooked rice). Bake in the oven at 170°C (325°F), Gas mark 3 for 12 minutes, before carefully removing the baking beans and the paper and baking the case for another 15 minutes or until the pastry is cooked through and a light golden colour. (Small individual tarts will need less time – see page 23.) Allow to cool before adding the filling.
- Some of the whoopie pie recipes need the batter to be rested in the fridge before cooking. The resting time varies, but in fact the mixture can be kept in the fridge for up to 1 day. However, do be careful not to refrigerate for any longer than this, or you might find that the whoopie pies don't rise very much.

Finally, don't forget to have fun and to enjoy sharing your scrumptious homemade cakes!

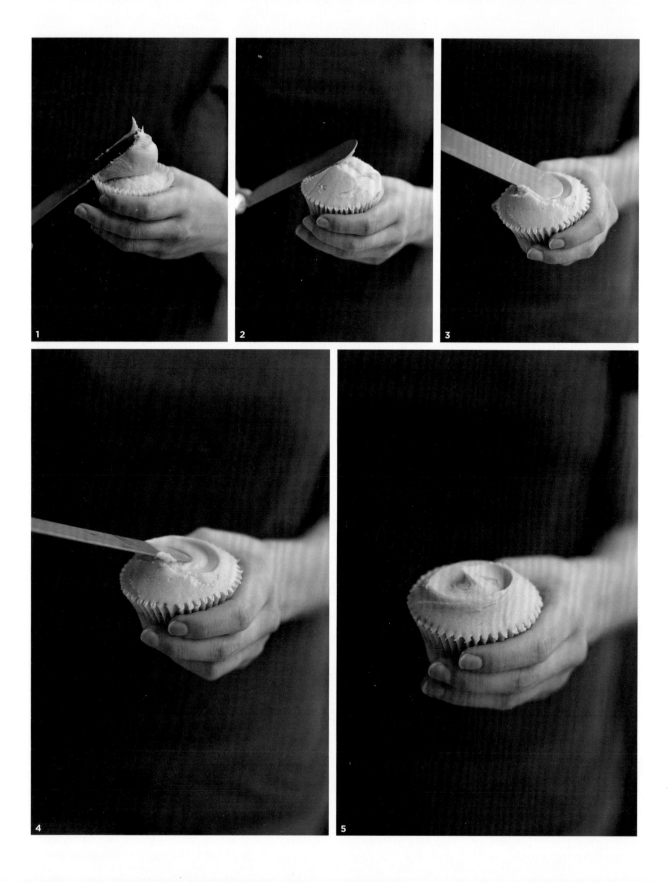

FROSTING CUPCAKES

1. Use a palette knife to place a generous amount of frosting on top of the cupcake.

2. With the flat surface of the palette knife, spread the frosting around the top of the cake, smoothing downwards and making sure it covers all the way to the edge of the paper case.

3. Put the flat tip of the palette knife in the centre and move in a circular motion to make an indented swirl in the frosting.

4. To create a pretty peak on top, lift the palette knife upwards at the last second.

5. Now enjoy your gorgeous Hummingbird cupcake with its perfect swirled frosting. If you wish, sprinkle over the decoration of your choice, such as coloured strands.

FROSTING LAYER CAKES

1. Place the first layer of sponge on a board or plate. With a palette knife, smooth a generous amount of frosting onto the sponge, making sure it is evenly spread and almost reaches the edges. Place the second sponge layer on top and smooth on the frosting as you did for the first layer.

2. Add the third sponge layer in the same way. (If you're making one of our four-layer cakes, the third sponge layer will need to be topped with frosting and the fourth layer added too.) Then lightly frost the sides of the cake. This is just a 'base coat' to pick up any loose crumbs.

3. Also give the top of the cake a light base coat of frosting. Now frost the sides and the top of the cake again, this time with a thicker layer of frosting; it should be thick enough that you can't see any of the sponge through the frosting.

4. Using the flat tip of the palette knife, add texture to the sides of the cake by gently pulling the palette knife upwards, from bottom to top, to create lines in the frosting.

5. Again using the flat tip of the palette knife, create the pattern on the top of the cake by starting from the outside edge and pulling the knife over the frosting and into the middle in gentle curved lines.

1

2

3

4

5

DECORATING IDEAS

When it comes to decorating your Hummingbird cakes, the possibilities are endless. You can keep things simple and understated, or you can have fun with different finishes and themes. Most of the recipes in this book include suggestions on how to decorate the cakes beautifully, but of course you might have your own ideas, or you can mix and match between recipes depending on the event or occasion. A huge variety of shop-bought decorations are available, or you may decide to make some by hand. Here are a few extra suggestions and tips to help inspire gorgeous decorations for your cakes.

EDIBLE SHAPES

You can decorate your cakes with edible shapes that reflect a particular theme or occasion. There are many shop-bought edible shapes available or you can make your own from sugarpaste (see instructions below). Whether you want tiny flowers for summery cupcakes, balloons on your birthday treats or snowmen to adorn a Christmas cake, just let your imagination guide you. Here are some suggestions.

Hearts

Stars

Balloons

Numbers or alphabet shapes

Flowers

Fruit (such as strawberry
    shapes or bunches of cherries)

Easter eggs

Animals (such as chicks,
    rabbits or reindeer)

Snowmen

Snowflakes

Christmas trees

Holly leaves

HAND-MADE SHAPES FROM SUGARPASTE OR READY-TO-ROLL ICING

Some of the cakes in the photographs (and in our bakeries) are finished with cut-out shapes that have been hand-made from sugarpaste or ready-to-roll icing. Specialist cake-decorating stores sell sugarpaste, colourings, and a variety of themed cutters. If you can't get the exact cutter you need, perhaps create a stencil to cut around, or do your best to cut out shapes freehand using a small, sharp knife.

Makes approximately 40 decorations (depending on cutter size)

- Soften about 50g (1¾oz) ready-to-roll sugarpaste or Regal Ice by working it into a ball between your hands.
- If you want to add colour, use gel or paste colourings to give the best results. (These can be bought online or from specialist cake-decorating stores.) Add the colouring in very small amounts until you achieve the shade you want. After each addition, work the colouring into the sugarpaste until the

colour is smooth and even. It's best to wear latex gloves when doing this or it can stain your hands.

- The sugarpaste is ready to be rolled out when it is soft, smooth and no longer sticky. Lightly dust a smooth surface with cornflour. Break off a small ball of the icing, place on the dusted surface and roll out gently with a smooth rolling pin to a thickness of 2–3mm (⅛in).
- Using your choice of shaped or themed cutters, carefully press out shapes from the sugarpaste. (Alternatively, use a small, sharp knife, but this is not as neat or accurate as using a cutter.)
- Once all the shapes have been cut out, use a tapered, angled palette knife to lift them carefully on to a tray lined with baking parchment. Leave the sugarpaste decorations to dry and harden overnight.
- When the sugarpaste shapes are dry you can decorate them further, if you wish, by dusting with shimmer, glitter or coloured lustre. Finally, position the shapes on top of your cake in whatever arrangement you fancy.

OTHER DECORATIONS AND FINISHES

Not everyone has access to a specialist cake-decorating store or enough time to hand-make shapes from sugarpaste. But there's a wealth of other simple solutions. Supermarkets sell a growing range of cake-decorating supplies, so have a look in the baking aisle. Many everyday ingredients can also be turned into pretty finishes that will make your cakes beautiful and professional-looking. Remember that different types of cakes suit different finishes, so try to use something that will complement the flavour, colour or style of the cake, and be guided by the ingredients in the recipe wherever possible.

Dusting of icing sugar, cocoa powder or cinnamon
Coloured or chocolate sprinkles
Edible glitter
Gold or silver dragées/balls
Chocolate chips
Grated or shaved chocolate
Drizzled melted chocolate
Chocolate coffee beans
Whole chocolates, such as Maltesers or truffles
Sugar-coated mini eggs
Sweets, such as jelly beans, mini gems or cola bottles
Toffee pieces
Crystallised fruit or petals (see page 248)

Candied peel or petals
Fresh fruit, whole or in slices
Mint leaves or thyme sprigs
Grated lemon or lime zest
Whole or half nuts, such as hazelnuts, walnuts or pecans
Scattering of flaked almonds or chopped nuts
Caramelised nuts (see page 248)
Shavings of fresh coconut (toasted if you like – see page 27)
Scattering of cake crumbs or crushed biscuits
Tinned caramel or *dulce de leche*
Piped coloured frosting (add your choice of colouring to the vanilla frosting on page 92)

CRYSTALLISED FRUITS, PETALS AND LEAVES

Fruits, petals and leaves look fabulous when they've been crystallised. (For an example, see the Honey and Pear Layer Cake on page 224). This impressive finish is often seen on professional cakes, but in fact it is very easy to do at home. Rose petals are particularly pretty when crystallised.

- Whisk 1–2 egg whites in a bowl until frothy. Prepare a second bowl with a generous amount of caster sugar.
- Dip your chosen fruits, petals or leaves into the frothy egg white so that the items are completely covered, then roll or press into the caster sugar (turning leaves and petals over so that both sides get coated). The sugar crystals will stick to the egg white.
- Place the crystallised items on a tray lined with baking parchment and allow to dry out overnight before using them to decorate your cakes.

CARAMELISED NUTS

Nuts are ideal on top of a cake, but to make them a little more indulgent and unusual, you could first caramelise them. For example, see the Courgette, Walnut and Cinnamon Layer Cake on page 95, which is topped with caramelised walnut halves. If you are caramelising small nuts, such as hazelnuts or almonds, leave them whole; larger nuts like walnuts and pecans are better as halves.

- Place the nuts on a baking tray lined with baking parchment.
- Place 200g (7oz) caster sugar in a small saucepan and cover with about 4 tablespoons of water.
- Set over a medium heat to melt the sugar, then boil for about 10 minutes until the mixture becomes a rich golden-brown caramel. Remove the pan from the heat.
- Use a spoon to carefully place a small amount of caramel over each nut, making sure it is completely covered.
- Leave the coated nuts to set for about 10–15 minutes before using.

SUPPLIERS

JANE ASHER PARTY CAKES
A wide range of baking, decorating and sugarcraft supplies, available from their online store or London shop. Worldwide delivery offered.

www.janeasher.com
+44 (0)20 7584 6177
Shop address: 22–24 Cale Street, London, SW3 3QU

FUNKY MUFFIN
Creative homebaking supplies – great for cupcake and muffin cases. Their online store offers UK delivery or a collection service for local customers (based in Surrey).

www.funkymuffin.co.uk
+44 (0)1483 799 140

CAKES, COOKIES & CRAFTS
A huge selection of baking and sugarcraft supplies, including tins, cutters, palette knives, edible decorations and more. Order online for UK or international delivery. They also offer a local collection service (based in Lancashire).

www.cakescookiesandcraftsshop.co.uk
+44 (0)1524 389684

THE CAKE SHOP
Stocks a good selection of decorations, cutters, cases and sugarcraft tools.

+44 (0)1865 248691
Shop address: 123–7 Avenue Four, The Covered Market, Oxford, OX1 3DZ

KNIGHTSBRIDGE PME
This online store stocks professional sugarcraft tools and a wide selection of bakeware and cake-decorating equipment. The sole UK distributor of products from US manufacturer Wilton; they also stock many good-quality British products. This is the supplier we use for all the Hummingbird bakeries.

www.cakedecoration.co.uk
+44 (0)20 3234 0049

HOME CHOCOLATE FACTORY
Specialising in supplies for homemade chocolates, this is where we source our essential oils and essences.

www.homechocolatefactory.com
+44 (0)20 8450 1523

SODA STREAM
The online SodaStream store is a great place to buy the flavoured syrups used in our soda cupcakes, such as cola, lemonade and orangeade syrup.

www.sodastream.co.uk
+44 (0)845 601 0093

INDEX

ABOUT THE AUTHOR

The Hummingbird Bakery first opened on London's Portobello Road in 2004. Owner Tarek Malouf wanted to introduce Londoners to the joys of authentic American baking – gorgeous cupcakes, moist layer cakes, delicious pies and fluffy buttercream icing. Hummingbird became an instant success. Now a London favourite, The Hummingbird Bakery has two other branches, in South Kensington and Soho, with a fourth branch due to open in 2011. There are also plans for an international franchise.

Tarek Malouf grew up in London and studied at university in London and Los Angeles. He then worked for America's ABC News network, before deciding to leave journalism to pursue an exciting business idea. Tarek had noticed that the range of indulgent cakes and bakes loved by Americans was almost non-existent in the UK. He decided it was time to bring these treats to the British public. The Hummingbird Bakery was born! This is the second cookbook from The Hummingbird Bakery.

ACKNOWLEDGEMENTS

A big 'thank you' to Heath MacIntyre for coming up with 100 fantastic new recipes for this book, and for all your hard work and dedication since 2004. It has been a pleasure working with you over the years and, wow, we've come a long way since those early days at Portobello Road! Thank you to Emma Power, Hummingbird's Product Development Manager, for bringing your experience and creativity and lifting our offerings sky high! Your input into this book and your support for Heath has been invaluable. Thanks also to Sue Thedens for creating Hummingbird's company graphics and identity, which has evolved beautifully over the years.

Thanks to Lizzy Gray, Ione Walder and Myfanwy Vernon-Hunt at HarperCollins, and to Joss Herd, Kate Whitaker, Lucy McKelvie and Liz Belton for being so enthusiastic, creative and supportive whilst putting together *Cake Days*, and for creating a book so beautiful while remaining true to the Hummingbird brand. Thank you to my agent Zoë Waldie at Rogers, Coleridge and White for your guidance in bringing me to HarperCollins.

Finally, as always, I'm very grateful to all the wonderful Hummingbird Bakery staff past, present and future – your hard work has made Hummingbird what it is today!

First published in 2011 by Collins
an imprint of HarperCollins*Publishers*
77–85 Fulham Palace Road
London W6 8JB

www.harpercollins.co.uk

9 8 7 6 5
15 14 13 12 11

Photography © Kate Whitaker, 2011
Text © Tarek Malouf and The Hummingbird Bakery, 2011

Senior Commissioning Editor: Lizzy Gray
Editorial: Ione Walder and Kate Parker
Design: Myfanwy Vernon-Hunt and Lee Motley
Styling: Joss Herd, Lucy McKelvie and Liz Belton

Tarek Malouf asserts his moral right to be identified
as the author of this work.
A catalogue record for this book is available from the British Library.

ISBN: 978-0-00-737479-3

Printed and bound by Butler Tanner & Dennis Ltd, Frome